Philippe Wolff, ~~~~~~~~~~~~~~~~~~~~~~~ ral
History at the ~~~~~~~~~~~~~~~~~~~~~~~ is
awarded the Pr~~~~~~~~~~~~~~~~~~~~~ of
Toulouse (1958), ~~~~~~~~~~ the author of *The
Awakening of Europe* (1968), among many other
books and articles. He died in September 2001 at
the age of 88.

Western Languages

AD 100–1500

PHILIPPE WOLFF

Translated from the French by
Frances Partridge

PHOENIX

A PHOENIX PAPERBACK

First published in Great Britain in 1971
by George Weidenfeld & Nicolson Ltd
This paperback edition published in 2003
by Phoenix,
an imprint of Orion Books Ltd,
Orion House, 5 Upper St Martin's Lane,
London WC2H 9EA

A CIP catalogue record for this book
is available from the British Library.

ISBN 1 84212 276 2

Typeset at The Spartan Press Ltd,
Lymington, Hants

Printed and bound in Great Britain by
Clays Ltd, St Ives plc

CONTENTS

List of abbreviations   vi

1 Introduction   1
2 Remote origins   21
3 The period of formation   42
4 The Tower of Babel   80
5 Crystallisation   104
6 From Dante to Caxton, Luther and Nebrija   149
7 Conclusion   180

Notes   188
Bibliography   189
Acknowledgments   193
Index   195

List of abbreviations

arag.	=	Aragonese
cast.	=	Castilian
cat.	=	Catalan
eng.	=	English
fr.	=	French
ger.	=	German
got.	=	Gothic
h.	=	High (h. ger. = High German)
ind. eur.	=	Indo-European
icel.	=	Icelandic
it.	=	Italian
lat.	=	Latin
occ.	=	Occitan (used in preference to Provençal)
o.	=	Old
o. h. ger.	=	Old High German
pied.	=	Piedmontese
port.	=	Portuguese
rom.	=	Romanian
s.	=	Saxon
sp.	=	Spanish

> between two terms means that the second developed from the first

* denotes a word of which no written trace remains, but which has been reconstructed from later derivations

Chapter One

INTRODUCTION

It is strange that until the present day historians have
paid scant attention to this type of [linguistic] community
and hardly noticed its great significance and decisive
effect on the future history of man.

WALTER VON WARTBURG, *Problems and Methods of Linguistics*

DO NOT SPEECH and writing play a fundamental part in man's
activities? Social life is inconceivable without some system of
signs enabling men to communicate with each other, and
language soon established itself as the chief of these signs.

In our own time, more than a milliard of the three and a
half milliards of the earth's inhabitants habitually and officially
speak and write languages derived from those formed in
Europe during the first fifteen centuries of our era.

These banal and obvious reflections stress the fact that it is a
historian's duty to concern himself with linguistic data, and
that those of the period we now call the Middle Ages are of
particular interest. Indeed he cannot have ignored them, at
least on certain occasions when their importance has been
especially evident. Any history of the 'great invasions', the
Völkerwanderung, must contain a chapter devoted to their
linguistic consequences, to the losses of *Romania*, and the
adoption of Latin by the 'Barbarians' who had settled on the
soil of the Empire. Latin evolved rapidly, however, and it was a
historian, Ferdinand Lot, who was one of the first to try and
answer the question: when did men stop talking Latin? Marc
Bloch, the historian of feudal society, has successfully shown
the part played by linguistic usage in the formation of social

and juridical concepts between the tenth and twelfth centuries. The conquest of the Anglo-Saxon countries by William the Conqueror and his French-speaking knights had effects on the language which have been carefully studied by British historians as well as linguists. All these aspects, and others besides, have been noticed, but never integrated in a complete linguistic history of medieval Europe.

Linguists, for their part, have accumulated a mass of material of the greatest interest to historians. In their search for the external causes of the development of language they have had to take an increasingly exact account of historical situations, and of social structures and their development. Works like that of the late W. D. Elcock (*The Romance Languages*, London, 1960), or the two volumes so far published of Hans Eggers' history of the German language (*Deutsche Sprachgeschichte*, 1963–5), to mention but two, go in for analyses that are extremely subtle and in the highest degree suggestive to the historian. But their viewpoint naturally remains linguistic.

The historian's point of view is necessarily different. He projects his mind into a chosen historical setting: a certain country or group of countries at a certain period. He is often concerned with languages belonging to quite distinct groups, such as the Romance and Germanic languages. He makes use of very different comparisons from those of the linguist. They are directed at the human groups which transmit these languages. And he is not so much interested in the linguistic data as such, as in the attitude to them of the men he is studying. How did linguistic data figure in their concepts of man and the universe? What problems were set them by the diversity of languages? How far did they get in analysing these phenomena? The historian has to work out a synthesis of all these aspects.

Linguistic history offers the historian a very unusual opportunity: to make contact with documentary material produced not by a few fairly intelligent and representative individuals, but by the 'articulate masses'. Linguistic innovations are all the time being tried out, or at least diffused among large groups. Analysis of the state of a language involves studying the phonetic and grammatical habits of hundreds of thousands or even millions of persons, and the stock of words at their disposal. This social aspect is one of the elements that defines a language, and must be of the deepest interest to a historian. He can hope to gain from it a better knowledge of human societies, their development and mental processes.

But his way is beset with difficulties, which probably explains the lack of headway he has made so far. The documentation is of exceptional interest, but we must not forget that it is also incomplete. Linguistic evolution in the past – particularly in medieval Europe – is only accessible to us through written documents. But writing is a curiously distorting mirror, and the symbols have often ceased to correspond with the sounds they at first represented. The difference between the spoken and written language may even amount to almost complete divorce: as, for instance, during the centuries when Latin was still almost the only written language in Europe, while the spoken languages had become to a large extent emancipated. Lastly, only an infinitesimal number of these documents have come down to us, especially for the crucial period – the first thousand years after Christ, when communities were beginning to be aware of their increasing linguistic differences. These were centuries of ignorance, or of very feeble culture, during which language developed in almost complete freedom, but which, for the same reason, left behind very little written evidence. Linguists must make every effort to overcome or avoid these obstacles, and historians depend on their failures as much as on their successes.

The more complete history tries to be, the less it lies within the scope of an individual. As soon as it begins burrowing beneath the surface of events, it calls upon multiple skills, each so demanding that they exclude one another almost fatally. How is it possible to be an economist, a jurist, a theologian and a psychologist at the same time? The need to acquire a sound knowledge of linguistics after having already absorbed the basic disciplines of history has probably made many historians draw back. Those who advance should learn modesty from these facts, as the author of this book is well aware. But it is time to make a start.

On the threshold of this work, which is primarily intended not for linguists but for historians and anyone interested in history, some slight initiation into linguistics seems necessary. But I shall try not to discourage my readers and keep it to a minimum. Ferdinand de Saussure, who played an important part in the development of modern linguistics, distinguished several aspects: synchronic linguistics, or the analysis of the state of the language at a given moment, and the logical and psychological relations existing between terms, all from a static point of view; diachronic linguistics, or the study of the evolution of language and the relations between successive terms; and geographical linguistics, which examines the relation of the linguistic phenomenon with space. These two last points of view evidently concern the historian, nor can he ignore the first. In the same way, economic history gains enlightenment from a combined study of the combination of events with an analysis of economic structures.

The synchronic aspect

Let us imagine an individual at the moment of expressing himself: his mind contains a whole collection of associations between concepts and auditory images. This is what we call language: it is a social product, learned in the heart of the community in which he lives. He has assimilated it more or less completely and precisely: his vocabulary is more or less rich, his knowledge of grammar more or less sound. But beneath these individual differences lies the accumulated treasure which is the truly 'social part' of language. Now he begins to speak, thus performing an act of will and intelligence: he chooses a certain number of combinations to express his personal thoughts, and these make up his conversation. But he also brings into play a certain number of nerves and muscles to make his utterance audible. If this psycho-physical element of speech is not activated, his remarks remain as thoughts in his mind. The individual may also choose to express his remarks in writing. Writing is another system of signs, but without autonomy of its own, since its purpose is to represent language; it is also true to say that it is a distorted image, and difficulties of orthography account for these distortions.

This short analysis has brought us closer to the extremely complex notion of speech, and enabled us to isolate it from the notion of language. As Saussure said: 'La langue est pour nous le langage moins la parole' ('Language is speech without words'). For there to be language, a linguistic community must exist, a large or small group of human beings who share it in common: this social aspect is really one of its innate characteristics. Language, thus defined, is the object of linguistics.

Let us begin by determining what constitutes such a linguistic system, or 'state of language' as it is called, within a given human group and a space of time sufficiently short for only minimal modifications to intervene. This is the true field of study of synchronic linguistics.

Phonetics One branch is devoted to studying the sonorous material used by language. It is not the same in all languages, as is sufficiently proved by the difficulties we all have in pronouncing a foreign tongue. This branch is generally known as phonetics.

In conversation, the auditory impression enables us to distinguish the sounds making up the spoken chain. It has been shown that the same sound **b** invariably corresponds to the same act of articulation **bl**: this combination is described as a 'phoneme', in reference only to the special characteristics which distinguish it from all other combinations.

Sounds are produced by a somewhat complicated activity of the vocal apparatus, which cannot be described in detail here. The air expelled by the lungs flows through this apparatus, and these sounds are varied by the combined activity of its parts. Thus one may briefly distinguish:

Vowels corresponding to the widest opening of the buccal cavity. These are usually voiced, that is to say produced by vibration of the vocal cords. The semivowels (i, u, ü) depend on a smaller aperture, not much larger than that for consonants. Then we have e, o, ö – which can be either shut or open in many languages. A is the most open of the vowels.

Consonants depending on the buccal cavity being more or less closed. Other factors beside the degree of closure are involved in their classification: the place and the manner of articulation, the vibration or absence of vibration of the vocal cords.

Lastly, vowels and consonants can be oral if the air is expelled by the mouth alone; or nasal if the uvula allows some of the air to pass through the nasal cavity. And they can also be either long or short.

But the phonetician cannot confine himself to describing and classifying phonemes. These units must take their place in those 'stretches of spoken sounds', among which the simplest is the syllable (even though it is difficult to define it scientifically). We say that a syllable is open if it ends with a vowel (which is then said to be free); and closed if it ends with a consonant, in which case the vowel is enclosed by the group formed by this consonant and the first consonant in the succeeding syllable. We must also introduce the idea of the diphthong, or combination of two vowels pronounced in a single emission of the voice while preserving the duality of the sound.

After the syllable, we come naturally to the next unit – the word: a piece of sonorous material representing a certain concept. The scientific definition of a word raises numerous difficulties, but it does not seem possible to do without this very useful notion.

Classification of the consonants (simplified table)

1 Buccal cavity completely closed: occlusives.
   According to the place of articulation, these are:
      labials (p, b, m): articulated with the lips together;
      dentals (t, d, n): the tip of the tongue is pressed against the front of the palate;
      gutturals (k, g, ṅ): the back of the tongue is in contact with the back of the palate.
   Each group possesses one unvoiced sound (p, t, k), formed without any vibration of the vocal cords; one voiced sound (b, d, g), with vibration; and one nasal (m, n, ṅ) in which some of the air passes through the nasal cavity.
2 Very slight opening of the buccal cavity: spirants (or fricatives; in allusion to the impression of friction produced by the expulsion of the air). The following can be distinguished:
      affricates: a combination of occlusive and fricative types (tch in the English *chair*, ts);
      labiodentals (f, v): with the lower lip and teeth close together.
      according to the position of the tip of the tongue, the inter-dentals (þ, đ, corresponding respectively with the English th in *thing* and *the*), the sibilants (s, z), hushing sounds (š, ž, corresponding to the French sounds *chant*, *génie*);
      the palatals and gutturals (corresponding to the German sounds: *ich*, *liegen*, or *Bach*, *Tage*).
3 Wider opening of the buccal cavity: liquids.
   According to the movement of the tongue, lateral articulation (l, palatal or liquid), and vibrant articulation (r) can be distinguished. L and r are generally voiced.

Inside the word there is an accent, normally depending on intensity. The speaker articulates the accented syllable more forcefully than the rest. The place of this accent in the word differs according to language, but is more or less regularly fixed. Its strength may vary too: it is much weaker in French than in the Germanic languages or Italian, for instance – which has led to many difficulties for Frenchmen learning to speak these languages. But there also once existed a musical, melodic accent: the voice was raised a quarter or a fifth of a tone higher when articulating the accented syllable.

After these units of syllable and word, the greatest attention must be given to the connection between articulated sounds, or what might be called the 'phonology of groups'. This is of capital importance when we move on to diachronic phonetics, or the study of the evolution of sounds.

Lexicology The linguist next enters the domain of lexicology and is at once struck by a distinction. Let us take a sentence at random: 'The father has just eaten his meal'. Among the words that make it up, some carry a full quota of meaning, such as 'father', 'eaten', 'meal'. Each of these, taken alone, corresponds to a certain concept and can be called full words. Others, on the contrary, have only a grammatical part to play in the sentence: these are form-words, in this case 'the', or 'his'. This distinction closely connects the study of words with that of grammar.

Let us now take a simple word from one of the languages of antiquity. We find three elements in it, always placed in the same order. For instance the Greek verb *zeúgnūmi* meaning 'I yoke':

This verb is conjugated: *zeúgnūmi, zeúgnūs, zeúgnūsi* etc. At the end of the word therefore, we find a variable ending, *-mi, -s, -si*, indicating the role of the word in the sentence.

The rest of the word, *zeúgnu-* is what is called the root, or inflective stem. But a more exact examination enables us to break it down into a suffix – *nū* – characteristic of the verbal form, and also found in *deikhnūmi*, *òrnūmi* etc, and an irreducible root, *zeug-*, which contains the indeterminate idea of 'to yoke'. We find it again in the word '*zeugma*', for instance, meaning a yoke, this time with a substantival suffix susceptible of receiving the terminations that form a declension.

The stem is thus the word without the inflective termination; but the root is the irreducible element within the stem, expressing the concept in its most indeterminate form.

These elements are seen in all Indo-European languages. In German the root is usually monosyllabic, and often allows of vowel changes (*werd-*, *wird-*, *wurd-*). In French there are very few changes of this sort; the root is very variable in aspect. While the suffix is the component part that is placed after the root to form the stem, all these languages also use prefixes, which precede the stem and modify its meaning (i.e. *hupo-zeúgnūmi* 'to put under the yoke').

The definition of a prefix brings us to the composition of words. Every language makes compound words by grouping together simple ones in different ways. German is particularly noted for its capacity to make compound words, and an intelligent individual can always invent them for himself.

Substantives are endowed with gender, naturally or otherwise. At first, masculine gender was given to all male living creatures, feminine gender to females, and neuter to the rest. Animistic tendencies explain the attribution of masculine or feminine to inanimate entities such as the Earth, rivers, etc, whence analogies between the meanings of words have had the effect of extending these categories of masculine and feminine in a more or less arbitrary fashion. The Germanic languages have kept the neuter gender, whereas in the Romance languages it has been almost entirely abandoned, and the arbitrariness of gender is much in evidence: why do we say *le banc* and *la chaise*? There is a historical explanation, but none in terms of their meanings.

Every word carries a meaning: as we have said earlier, it is a piece of sonorous material representing a concept. But it is not enough to correlate sounds and ideas. The French word *mouton* means the same as the English word *sheep*: but if one of these animals is killed and part of it is cooked and served up at table, a Frenchman will still call it *mouton*, while an Englishman speaks of *mutton*. A linguist would say that *mouton* means the same as *sheep*, but does not have the same value, because in certain cases covered by the same word in French, the Englishman uses a different word. The value of a word is thus determined by its relations with neighbouring words. Semantics is the study not only of meanings but of the values of words; it also examines their evolution, or their diachronic aspect.

The example just given suggests that the English language has a richer vocabulary than French. In fact the first contains about 240,000 words, as against only 93,000 in the second (and 51,000 in Latin). This richness also depends on the degree of aptitude for absorbing foreign terms. Such lexical creations constitute one of the most superficial features of a language. But lexical richness and the degree of subtlety of semantic analysis correspond to profound psychological tendencies.

Grammatical systems We come finally to the grammatical system of a language, which is determined by the relations between the words in a sentence. Classically, a distinction is made between morphology, which concerns the form of words – that is to say both the category they belong to (substantive, adjective, verb), and the form of their inflexion (declension, conjugation) – and syntax, which takes account both of the role of the order of words in the construction and arrangement of the sentence, and includes the rules of subordination and types of expression (affirmative, interrogative, exclamatory). These two aspects are in fact closely connected, and are best considered together. We cannot even separate them completely from lexicology, since certain languages rely upon form-words to express relations that others keep for inflexion.

It is here that we come up against a fundamental distinction. Languages have various ways of expressing the functions of words and the relationships between them:

One is modification of the root, already mentioned. Thus the Indo-European root *men-* can appear in the forms of *men-*, *mon-*, and even *mn-* (zero degree – no vowel). Modification was used in Latin. It is still important in the Germanic languages (e.g. in German, the conjugation: *brechen*, *brach*, *gebrochen*).

Another is the addition of terminations after the stem, thus affecting the end of the word: the use of these terminations is what is properly known as the inflexion of the word. In Indo-European, inflexion was general. It has been to a greater or lesser extent preserved in the languages derived from it.

Finally, there is the use of form-words, such as articles, some pronouns and prepositions. A language which uses such words extensively is called analytic. French has kept certain inflexions (as in the verb: *garde*, *gardons*, *gardez*). However, the system has been simplified, and the personal pronoun must now be used: *je garde*, *il garde*, where Latin merely used inflexion: *servo*, *servat*. In the same way, while Latin terminations are often sufficient to indicate gender (*rosa*, *dominus*), the article must be added in French: *la chaise*, *le meuble*. Moreover, while inflexion suffices to indicate the function of the substantive in Latin, '*rosam cepit*', French also makes use of the order of the words: '*il prit la rose*'.

This account is in no way complete, but it makes it possible to distinguish between an inflected and an analytic language. A distinction of first importance for our exposition, because the part played by inflexion in the languages that originated in medieval Europe diminished to make way for an increase in analysis and the use of form-words.

It is one of the most profound changes with which we shall be concerned.

The diachronic aspect

The synchronic study of language may give us a misleading impression of fixity. It must always leave current modifications out of count. Languages alter with varying speed, but incessantly.

What is the nature of linguistic change? First of all we have phonetic changes, affecting only the phonic aspect of words. These are involuntary and unconscious, but none the less regular, and apply to all words containing the phoneme in given surroundings and with given accentuation. Thus, in modern German every *ī* has become *ei*: *wīn*, *trīben*, *līhen*, *zīt* have given us *Wein*, *treiben*, *leihen*, *Zeit*. But we must not forget that these changes are always connected with certain conditions of time and environment: the dialectal variations in the same language give sufficient proof of this. Gilliéron has even demonstrated that there is no absolute regularity within an environment, even if it is as restricted as a single village during a given period.

Many of these phonetic changes consist in dropping the phonemes at the end of words, or even whole syllables if unaccented. These disappearances contribute more than any other factor to create what is the usual effect of phonetic changes: they interrupt the normal functioning of the grammatical system, the links between terms or the composition of words. The loss of the final *-m* alters the whole system of inflexion characteristic of Latin. Who would recognise in the French words *maison* and *ménage* the Latin vocables (*mansionem, mansionaticum*) from which they were derived? It was easy to analyse the Middle German word *dritteil* (= third + part, *Teil*); today the words *Teil* and *Drittel* seem to have no connection with each other. Phonetic evolution is a potent and constant cause of confusion.

To re-establish consistency in a language that has been disturbed in this way, linguistic communities make use of the extremely widespread process of analogy. For example: in Latin, *honōsem* originally corresponded to the nominative form *honōs*. Then the *s* was rhotacised, and the word became *honōrem*. Phonetic development thus duplicated the root. Regularity was re-established thanks to the creation of the nominative *honor*, by analogy with *ōrātor, ōrātōrem*. Analogy thus consists in the creation of a form similar to another, or to several others, according to definite rules.

The process of analogy is related both to phonetics and morphology. It may be purely morphological, as when, in the present indicative of the French verb *aimer*, an *e* was added to *j'aim* (derived from *amo*), by analogy with *tu aimes, il aime*. However, in this strictly morphological domain, some forms persist and become anomalous as a language develops. Thus, the third person plural of the present indicative of the verb *to be* differs from the singular in Latin (*est/sunt*) just as in German ((*er*) *ist*/(*sie*) *sind*): it is a form derived from an old Indo-European verb. An anomaly of this sort obviously points the way to an ancient form.

Of course many changes take place in the domain of lexicology. At every period, to a greater or lesser extent, a language forms new words by borrowing from neighbouring languages, or even from an ancient one with which contact has been kept. But the meaning and value of the words themselves also develop, and their development is the concern of semantics.

Lastly there are subtler grammatical changes, of which Saussure gives an example in an excellent analysis:

Indo-European had no prepositions; the relationships they indicate were expressed by a great many highly significant cases. Nor were there compound verbs made with verbal prefixes, but only particles, little words added to a sentence to make the verb more exact and subtle . . . This was also true of primitive Greek: 1 *óreos baínō káta: óreos baínō* by itself means 'I come from the mountain', the genitive having the value of an ablative; *káta* adds the nuance: 'downhill'. At another period it would have been 2 *katà óreōs baíno*, with *katà* playing the part of a preposition, or again 3 *kata-baínō óreos*, combining the verb and particle, now a verbal prefix.

Here we have two or three distinct phenomena, all depending on one interpretation of the units: 1 The creation of a new sort of word, prepositions, merely by displacing the given units. A special order, of no significance originally and perhaps derived from some chance factor, permits of a new grouping: *katà*, at first independent, is joined to the substantive *óreos*, and this combination is again joined to *baínō* as its complement; 2 Appearance of a new verbal type (*kata-baíno*); this is a new psychological grouping, favoured by the special distribution of units and consolidated by agglutination; 3 As a natural consequence: weakening of the termination in the genitive (*óre-os*); it is *katà* that now has to express the essential idea which was formerly marked by the genitive alone; the importance of the termination -*os* is therefore lessened. The germ of its future disappearance is in the phenomenon.[1]

It would be impossible to demonstrate more clearly the way in which phonetic and morphological change (dropping part or all of the termination) is in fact preceded by some psychological mutation that a superficial study would have overlooked. This prepares us to understand the complexity of the problem now confronting us:

What are the causes of linguistic change? We can dismiss the over-simple and once popular explanations relating to racial predisposition or adaptation to soil and climate.

It is a fact that a language evolves more rapidly during certain periods than others. In the case of a sufficiently developed civilisation, there are factors that put a brake on the evolution of the language: the Court or the Academy may react against it in the name of tradition, a cultured society may be influenced by education and literature. These are the brakes, but their activity is reduced or suppressed during periods of trouble or upheaval.

It is impossible to over-emphasise the importance of ethnic intermixing (so long as we eliminate pseudo-scientific racial considerations). A linguistic community is conquered by another nation, which imposes its superior civilisation: the community adopts that nation's language, while modifying it by habits of pronunciation, vocabulary and even grammar, for example, Gaul or the Iberian peninsula, conquered by the Romans. We call this the effect of the 'substratum'. The opposite case is when a linguistic community is invaded by a nation which merges with it and adopts its language with certain modifications, for example, Gaul or the Iberian peninsula invaded by the Germanic races, Franks, Visigoths, etc. This time we have to do with the effect of the 'superstratum' and in these circumstances, the effect of the bilingualism that persists and the effect of mixed marriages, will be noticed.

Lexicological changes are not very difficult to account for. It usually happens that, when an object or idea penetrates a linguistic community, the word that represented it in its community of origin is adopted with it. One is reminded in particular of words borrowed from a technical vocabulary, the religious vocabulary adopted with the spread of Christianity, and the propagation of scientific terms. The influence of fashion also plays a part. And within a language, certain words at least may suffer semantic wear and tear, so that new ones are looked for, in order to regain the value lost by the first.

We come next to strictly linguistic considerations, such as the influence of stress and what is called the law of least effort. The stronger and more concentrated the accent falling on certain syllables, the more do those that are little or not at all stressed tend to be reabsorbed or disappear. This rule holds also for the phenomena of assimilation. The transformation of the Latin *factum*, later *factu* into Italian *fatto* is a good example of both. But though this explanation is valid in some cases, it is not borne out by others:

> If it is maintained that the Slavonic shortening of *ā*, *ē* into *ă*, *ĕ* is due to the law of least effort, it must also be held that the inverse phenomenon presented by German (*făter > văter*, *gĕben > gēben*) is a case of the greater effort. If the sonant is easier to pronounce than the surd (cf. *opera > occ. obra*) the opposite ought to need a greater effort, yet in Spanish *z* has become *x* (cf. *hixo*, son, written *hijo*), and Germanic changes *b*, *d* and *g* into *p*, *t* and *k*.[2]

Lastly we come to grammatical changes. It would seem dangerous to see these as no more than secondary phenomena, or efforts to reconstruct the system of a language disturbed by phonetic evolution on new foundations. Was it solely because the dropping of final consonants upset the regularity of Latin declensions and conjugations that form-words were made use of and organised – articles, personal pronouns, and prepositions expressing what the missing terminations could no longer convey? Even if the two phenomena had occurred in this chronological order, it would be wrong to neglect two fundamental facts. First, that phonetic evolution is to some extent conditioned and prepared for by displacement or relaxation of grammatical interest (see the example given on page 14). Secondly, that the elaboration of a new system calls for a more or less unconscious combination of research and sharp-ened thought mechanisms. We can then accept the idea that a certain intellectual progress renders language a more and more exact and powerful instrument for man's use, and we may hope to retrace that progress by analysing this instrument. Thus we see language as 'the chief document of the spiritual history of humanity'.[3] At all events it is a matter of prime importance, particularly for historians.

Reconstitution How can retrospective diachrony reconsti-tute these developments and reconstruct vanished states of a language? A difficult problem for linguists! The only documentation they possess is written, and it always contains enormous lacunae, even in relatively favourable cases, like that bearing on the origins of the Romance languages. There is always the possibility of a gap between a written and spoken language. There is a whole series of phenomena, those in the domain of phonetics, for which we only have indirect evidence, difficult to decipher; linguists have to rely on guidance provided by poetry, with its rules of alliteration, assonance or rhythm.

Some languages disappeared without leaving any written trace. They can only be reconstructed, partially at least, by comparing the languages derived from them. This is the case with Indo-European: the inheritance common to all the languages derived from this stem enables some of its features to be re-established. Such parallels do not merely reveal common roots, but also the phonological system or even actual forms of Indo-European. For instance, it is thought that the first part of the Greek *állo* (other), and of the Latin *aliud* corresponds to an *a* which existed in Indo-European. From the fact that in Latin we have the form *aliud* (in opposi-tion to *bonum*), in Greek the form *állo* (derived from *allod* – as against *kalon*), and in English the form *that*, it has been deduced that in Indo-European the neuter singular termination for pronouns was -*d*, in opposition to the adjectival termination -*m*. Such conclusions, carefully amassed and collated, make it possible to reconstruct words that have vanished without leaving their trace on any document.

Geographical and social aspects

We now come to the external aspects of linguistics, which are of somewhat secondary interest to linguists but of capital importance to us. So far, we have spoken of a language as belonging to a linguistic community, whether at a given period or in its entire evolution. And we have argued mainly from countries like Italy, Spain, England etc, each with its own language. But things are not so simple. In each country we find differences, geographical and social:

1 On the geographical level, we find the notion of dialect, which the uninitiated often think of as a simple one. During the period under consideration, the phenomenon of dialect was essential. In practice, we are tempted to treat the dialects of a country as if they were separate linguistic forms – as if, for instance, there was a clearly defined dialect in Picardy, entirely different from the neighbouring dialects and separated from them by obvious frontiers. Unfortunately this is not so. As soon as one tries to define it, the phenomenon of dialect slips between one's fingers. Yet we cannot deny its existence. Perhaps it can be represented as follows.

   Within the territory of a linguistic community, linguistic evolution becomes increasingly divergent in proportion as the links between the groups composing it are loosened. Each innovation occurs in only one part of the region. Each has its own distinct area. If we try to superimpose these areas on a map we are left with an extremely complex arrangement, in which the limits of separate linguistic data cross one another in a confused way. Yet this diagram is the only one that is strictly accurate, for scientifically speaking there are no dialects, only dialectal characteristics. Either a dialect must be defined by the totality of its characteristics, and there are as many dialects as places (there may even be several in one village!), or else it is defined by only one, in which case the limits traced correspond to no dialectal reality.

This severe, but extremist position is probably not the best. The best (and one which linguists usually adopt) is to select a certain number of dialectal characteristics that are both typical and have somewhat similar limits, and so define ways of speech, that are fairly clearly differentiated. But it must never be forgotten that this notion of dialect is very indefinite and relative, and also that it corresponds to a region whose approximate frontiers are represented by lines that are only roughly adjacent. It might therefore be said that a dialect is a collection of ways of speech which, without being identical, present features in common and a general air of resemblance of which the speakers of it are aware.

As soon as a dialect prevails within a region, as soon as writing becomes important and continuous relationships develop between human groups, something superior to this dialect is created. Linguists speak of a 'force of intercourse', which opposes some local innovations and spreads others, so favouring the formation of a language of communication. The most diverse factors converge to affect it – political, economic and religious. A national language that has been thus unified invades the domains of administration, litera-ture, etc. A dialect that has failed to enter the domain of writing, ends as no more than a patois.

2 To follow this evolution, we have had to combine strictly human aspects with geographical ones, to speak of the level of civilisation, and of political, economic and religious

factors. In conclusion we must again insist on the very simple truth that language is always a social phenomenon, and that its evolution can only be properly understood in the light of a thorough analysis of social realities – realities which are, inversely, made accessible by such an analysis.

Linguistic reality, therefore, cannot be completely translated by a geographical map. Every individual contains several linguistic levels: the same man will speak his dialect (or patois) in moments of intimacy and abandon, his national language on certain very definite occasions, and a technical language when he is at work. The number and respective importance of these linguistic levels in the same individual vary from one society to another and from one degree of civilisation to another.

However incomplete and summary this introduction may seem, it should make it possible for us to embark on our subject. Let us try to establish its limits. We shall confine ourselves to the domains covered by the Romance and Germanic languages, even if we may happen to allude to events in Slavonic, Hellenic and Celtic regions. Our period will cover about 1,500 years: from the beginning of the Christian era to the year 1500 – that is to say from the age of classical Latin and proto-Germanic to the affirmation by the Pleiad, Caxton, Luther and others, of vigorous linguistic entities that had developed during this period. Within these spatial and temporal limits, what are the most important aspects of linguistic evolution? What do we learn from the study of the state of the language at different periods? What part have linguistic phenomena played in social evolution? To what extent have men been aware of them?

Chapter Two

REMOTE ORIGINS

BY ABOUT 2000 BC, from Hindustan to the Atlantic and from Scandinavia to the Mediterranean, different languages were being spoken that can be considered as forms of an earlier common tongue: this earlier language is known as Indo-European because of its wide geographical range.

It will doubtless never be possible to draw an exact and complete portrait of this common ancestor. The chief difficulty comes from the fact that the languages derived from it were only stabilised by writing very late in the day, after they had already undergone considerable evolution: only four linguistic groups are known to us through documents previous to the Christian era – these are Hittite, Indo-Aryan, Greek and Italic. The rest appeared much later. We must resign ourselves to making a partial and theoretical reconstruction of the state of the Indo-European language, without even being certain that it was ever spoken by any race.

The relationship between most of the European languages is nevertheless an important phenomenon and has certainly facilitated changes and borrowings. Of the dozen recognised branches (several of them extinct) of the Indo-European family, we will confine ourselves to mentioning half: Hellenic, represented by the dialects of ancient and modern Greek; Italic, derived from which are some dead branches (Umbrian and Oscan), but also Latin, source of all the Romance languages. Among Celtic languages, it is usual to distinguish Brythonic with which are connected not only *Gallic and *Cornish (both vanished, though at different dates) but also Welsh and Breton, and the Gaelic spoken in Ireland, Scotland and the Isle of Man. Nor is there any difficulty concerning Baltic, whence came old Prussian, Lettish and Lithuanian; Slavonic, with its southern, western and eastern branches; and finally Germanic.

Problems concerning Latin

We now seem to be treading on firmer ground. Latin is one of the branches of the Italic stem of Indo-European. It had been the language of the populations of Latium from at least the sixth century BC. The Roman conquest caused it to triumph over the whole of Italy, eliminating other branches of Italic, such as Umbrian and Oscan, and carried it to the very confines of the Roman Empire. However, in most of the eastern part of the Empire, Latin was hardly used except for administrative purposes, and languages that had been spoken before, particularly Greek, were successful in resisting it. We know Latin well through its abundant and varied literature, dating from the middle of the third century BC, the study of which still plays an important part in some forms of education today. The Romance languages were derived from Latin: Italian, Catalan, Spanish, Portuguese, French, Rhaeto-Romanic and Romanian. It will clearly be an essential part of our task to study the historical conditions of the development of these languages from Latin.

So far so good. But as soon as we try to dig deeper and be more exact, our problem reveals increasing complexities.

Between classical Latin, as it appears in literary texts, and our modern languages there is evidently a considerable difference. Latin is an inflected language, that is to say that the nature of the word and the part it plays in the sentence are normally indicated by its termination. Thus *dominus*, because it ends in *-us*, must be a substantive or an adjective. We know that it is a substantive, meaning 'master'. This termination varies with the part played by the word in the sentence. Take the sentence: *dominus cepit rosam*. The ending *-us* shows that it belongs to the subject, while *-am* indicates the direct object. As for the verb, *-it* corresponds to the third person singular. The meaning is clear: 'the master took the rose'. It would still be the same if the order of the words was changed: *rosam cepit dominus*.

The inflective system therefore gave Latin great freedom in the order of the words – subject to certain rules and usages. And the language took advantage of this freedom to emphasise words or produce literary effects. Thus the most important word might be placed either at the beginning or the end of the sentence. An example of the first type: *Legiones abducis a Bruto. Quas?* (Cicero): 'You are taking legions away from Brutus. Which?'. And of the second: *Ut in perpetua pace esse possitis, providebo* (Cicero): 'I shall make it possible for you to live in perpetual peace'. A translator is hard put to it to reproduce these effects in any of our modern languages: this is because their structure does not allow of comparable liberty.

There is another difference which at once strikes us in all these sentences: we can say with approximate accuracy that Latin uses far fewer words. Inflexion allows it to economise in a great many form-words, articles, pronouns and prepositions. One has only to think of the phrase *Eo rus* and try to translate it into a modern language: '*Je vais à la campagne*', 'I am going to the country', etc. The former gives an immediate impression of restraint and elegance (even if a more exhaustive study reveals that the absence of the article is in fact a sign of poverty).

This suppleness and elegance must, however, be paid for. The price is the extreme complication of the inflective system on which they depend. Substantives are declined like adjectives, and their declensions contain six cases in the singular and as many in the plural. There are no less than five types of declension, according to the last letter of the stem (*a, u, i* . . .), without counting irregular nouns. Three genders have also to be taken into account (masculine, feminine and neuter). A comparable analysis can likewise be made of the conjugations. Memorising these declensions and conjugations is usually the first task for students of Latin, and it is quite enough to put most of them off. Most modern European languages have simplified the system of conjugations; as for the declensions, either a few elements only are kept, or they are got rid of altogether.

The complexity of literary Latin is increased for us also by its syntax. The sentences in a literary Latin text are often long and complicated in construction, with clauses linked by different conjunctions in a good many different subordinate relationships. The syntax of most modern European languages is simpler, and phrases are placed side by side without a conjunction to separate them. This type of syntax does exist in classical Latin, but is not usual; it is deliberately employed to create a particular literary effect.

Thus in moving from a modern European language to literary Latin we get the impression of having changed worlds. The linguistic structures seem to differ profoundly. They may perhaps correspond to differences of traditional mental structure. We are therefore confronted by the historical questions: when did the transition from one type of structure to another take place? What historical phenomena, social mutations or intellectual transformations caused it? But the problem is at the same time simpler and more complicated than this.

We must first emphasise that the study of Latin literature cannot possibly give us a complete knowledge of the language, since we only know it through its written image. If methods of recording the human voice had existed in the times of Caesar and Cicero, we should have had the answer to a great many questions that perplex us today. We have some idea of the Latin vocalic and consonantal systems, since ancient grammarians have described them for us. We know in particular that each of the five Latin vowels could be long or short. A short vowel was as a rule pronounced more openly. This distinction was the basis of versification. But we are still extremely uncertain how Latin was pronounced in the 'classical' period – namely during the five or six centuries before and after the birth of Christ. It is rare today for any great international assembly to use spoken Latin as its working language. When this does happen, speakers find it extremely difficult to understand each other, not only because of their faulty pronunciation (or even knowledge) of Latin, but also because they have not all got the same idea of the sounds that issued from the mouths of Cicero or Virgil.

Another question: that of stress. Most linguists believe that the accent in Latin was intensive, that is to say that the accented syllable was more emphatically pronounced: this is the type of accent we know today. Others maintain that it was musical in character: the accented syllable was not pronounced more emphatically, but on a higher note. Some writers try to reconcile these two theories. The controversy is of interest, for it is accepted that the changes in spoken Latin after the third century AD were partly due to the habits of accentuation introduced by the barbarians when they began to speak Latin.

Even if we agree to consider Latin in the light of the image provided by its literature, this image is therefore incomplete, and some of the gaps in it are serious. Nor is this first reservation the most important we shall have to make.

Classical Latin and spoken Latin

Let us open volume four of the *Corpus Inscriptionum Latinarum*, which is entirely devoted to the very numerous graffiti found on the ruined walls of Pompeii. The population of this town was buried alive by the eruption of Vesuvius in AD 79, that is to say in a period considered classical from the language point of view. The exactness of the date is what interests us here. It proves that phenomena formerly thought to have occurred later, and taken for signs of the decadence of Latin, were already developing fully in the spoken language. Such was syncope, produced by the dropping of an unaccented vowel (*coliclo* for *cauliculum*, little cabbage); the substitution of *e* for *ae* or *oe* (*Phebus* for *Phoebus*), *o* for *au*; and above all the very common habit of discarding the final *-m*, which necessarily produced confusion in the declensions. Examples could be multiplied.

The other volumes in the same collection provide an abundance of inscriptions from tombs, both pagan and Christian, but often unfortunately undated. We cannot help feeling surprised when we decipher phrases such as: *Hic quescunt duas matres, duas filias, numero tres facunt.* (Here lie two mothers, two daughters, making three ... III, 3551, Pannonia); or *Hic requiiscunt menbra ad duus fratres Gallo et Fidencio* . . . (Here lie the limbs of the two brothers Gallus and Fidencius . . . XIII, 2483, Gaul.) The yod has been dropped from the verbs of the first inscription, the accusative is used for the nominative case, and the preposition *ad* is followed by the accusative to express possession (instead of the genitive): this last characteristic reminds one of an incorrect turn of phrase in modern French ('*les membres* AUX *deux frères*')!

Such tendencies were denounced by grammarians at a later date, as in the *Appendix Probi* of about the year 300 AD: syncope, dropping the final *-m*, throwing the system of declensions into confusion. It is interesting that all were operative by the first century AD, if not earlier.

Spoken Latin made a small place for itself in literature. A writer like Plautus (254–184 BC) who wrote comedies for a popular audience, deliberately adopted the mannerisms and tricks of speech of his hearers. He combed *ecce* (here, behold) with demonstrative pronouns (*ecca*, *eccilla*), a characteristic which reappeared much later in the Romance languages. He used the subjective personal pronoun with the verb, although the inflective system made this quite useless. He confused relative and interrogative pronouns. He assimilated the neuter gender to the masculine (*dorsus* for *dorsum*, back).

There is reason to believe that he exaggerated these habits, and ended by elaborating a rather artificial vulgar tongue. But all this must have had some foundation in reality, and it takes us back about two centuries before Christ. Even Cicero, who has been taken as the model writer of classical Latin ever since the time of the Carolingian humanists, deliberately adopted a familiar style in his letters. Thus he used a great many prepositions, far more than the 'genius of the language' dictated. He could have written that a certain man was *aptus alicui rei*, 'fitted for something', but instead he used a formula much closer to modern language (though not incorrect) and wrote *aptus ad aliquam rem* – a concession to the prepositional system which was finally to replace inflexion.

There is thus ample evidence for the existence of a spoken Latin, distinct from literary Latin, and we can even get some idea of what it was like. Latin writers were well aware of this; they distinguished *sermo rusticus* (rustic conversation) from *sermo urbanus* (polite or literary conversation). Modern linguists often talk of 'vulgar Latin', but the word contains a pejorative nuance that may be misleading. At all events its existence was of the first importance in the formation of the Romance languages, for they were derived from spoken and not from literary Latin. It is even possible, by means of a comparative study of modern Romance languages, to reconstruct certain aspects of this spoken Latin: thus fr. *cheval*, sp. *caballo*, it. *cavallo* indicate the existence of a common stem represented by the word **caballo*, the rustic equivalent of *equus*, which also appears in a writer like Horace, in the mocking sense of 'screw'. And specialists in the Romance languages like to give spoken Latin yet another name: as a natural result of their special viewpoint, they call it proto-Romance.

The problems that particularly concern us here are problems of nature, date and social differentiation.

Problems of nature: in what way, and to what extent, did spoken Latin differ essentially from written Latin? The elimination by literary Latin of so many current words that were considered familiar, vulgar or displeasing is a secondary matter. More important is the syntactic structure, that subordination of propositions one to another which establishes a sensitive hierarchy between ideas, at the same time as precise relationships between cause and effect. Most influential of all was probably the respect insisted upon by grammarians for the complicated system of inflexions, deployed within the compass of the declensions and conjugations. For it was this respect that preserved the originality of Latin in relation to most modern languages, and assured it the rich possibilities, the suppleness and elegance already referred to. One might of course say that the difference between literary and spoken Latin was above all a stylistic one, and that the former seems to have been a language to be used for 'noble' purposes, according to conservative criteria. This is to some extent true of all literary languages. But in the case of Latin, it is not only that the spoken language seems to have been imperfect. Just because literary Latin was so systematic and logical, spoken Latin compensated for its imperfections by making use of extremely different methods, which were to become general in the Romance languages.

Problems of date: are we justified in assuming that there was a golden age of classical Latin during the first century BC, with decadence beginning about the middle of the second century AD? If this chronology applies to literary Latin, does it also to spoken Latin? To what extent was the latter closer to literary Latin in the first century BC than later on? Can one talk of spoken Latin being decadent? It is very difficult to answer these questions, since our documentation of spoken Latin is particularly meagre for the first century BC; however, the examples from Pompeii prove that numerous characteristics traditionally attributed to later 'decadence' were to be found not far from Rome, and during the first century AD if not earlier.

Problems of social differentiation: one of the objections often made to the use of the formula 'vulgar Latin' is that it suggests that it was the means of expression of the so-called inferior classes of society, and theirs exclusively. This leads us into another problematic area, where we are once again without fixed landmarks. When Cicero arrived home after delivering one of his orations, exactly what sort of language did he speak? Was the Latin spoken by educated men close to literary Latin? And what proportion of the Latin-speaking population received even elementary education? From the second century BC to the third century AD did this proportion grow larger, or smaller? The social physiognomy of spoken Latin remains veiled in uncertainty and mystery.

It is tempting to say in conclusion that literary Latin was never spoken by anyone. A certain number of persons understood and appreciated it, and their daily conversation bore some resemblance to it. But it must have been a very small minority, and the Latin spoken by the masses always fell short of this ideal. And, starting from this assumption, it would seem that the transition from spoken Latin to the Romance languages did not involve such profound psychological mutations as those we think of connected with literary Latin. Rather is it a question of the very gradual promotion of a popular language to the rank of a literary language, with the centuries-long work of deepening, refinement and trial and error that such a phenomenon implies. But this could only happen under certain historical conditions. The development of the Romance languages from Latin was above all a social phenomenon.

Diversification of Latin

At first Latin was merely one of numerous languages in use in Italy. Only the Romans and the inhabitants of the small neighbouring region of Latium spoke it. This tribal speech must have been carried by the Roman conquest from the Scottish border to the Hellenistic Orient, and from present-day Romania to the pillars of Hercules, in spite of violent resistance from the vanquished races.

As soon as a region was conquered, the process of Romanisation began to develop in an almost uniform manner. The conquerors founded urban centres, whence they carried on the administration. These towns possessed schools where the pupils were taught in Latin, markets and places of amusement which attracted people from the surrounding countryside. Colonists from Italy, or men Romanised by service in the army, populated these towns, but they also settled in the country. This combination of circumstances produced a progressive spread of Latin from the towns into rural areas. Bilingualism became the rule, but the influence of Latin – the language of officialdom and culture – gradually prevailed. Finally, when a sufficient time had passed for this development to be completed, the indigenous language disappeared: this was the case in Gaul and the Iberian peninsula. Elsewhere, in Britain and the Danubian countries for example, Latin remained an urban language, and began to disappear with the decline of the towns in the third century AD.

In the Hellenic countries, which had been conspicuously urbanised since before the Roman conquest and possessed a cultural language even richer than Latin, the process was different. Greek prevented the spread of Latin towards the East, where it was only used in administration. The sole exception was Illyria, whence Latin was most probably carried into Dacia, north of the Danube. Greek played the part of substratum (see page 15) in the Greek colonies of Gaul, from

Nice to Ampurias, and in southern Italy, where it was still spoken to a large extent during the Middle Ages, (in 1368 Petrarch suggested that one of his secretaries should go to Calabria to improve his Greek), and where there are still a few Greek-speaking villages today. And Greek continued, above all, to be guardian of Latin, for Latin literature had imitated it as a cultural language and never stopped borrowing terms from it, even current ones. It is surely remarkable that the Greek word Πετρα should have triumphed over Latin *lapis*, and led to the it. *pietra*, rom. *piatră*, occ. *peira*, sp. *piedra* and fr. *pierre*, preserving *lapis* only in Italian and Spanish in the sense of 'tombstone'? This continuous influence of a co-existing language is what is known to linguists as that of the *adstratum*.

But the total disappearance of the indigenous vernacular in countries that had put up a desperate, brave and prolonged resistance to the Roman conquest, is worth some consideration. Although the evidence is scanty, all of it agrees in emphasising that these languages survived for a very long time. In Italy some of the graffiti at Pompeii are written in Oscan. In Spain, an author writing about AD 400 praises a Christian lady of Barcelona, for working hard to convert 'barbarians in soul and language' – presumably natives who were not yet Latinised. In Gaul, dedicatory inscriptions in Gallic ceased about the middle of the first century AD. But by the end of the fourth century, when St Jerome wrote his *Commentary on the Epistle to the Galatians*, he noted that the language of the Galatians was similar to that of the Treviri: a proof that Gallic was still spoken in the region of Trier, although it was an active centre of Romanisation. In the middle of the sixth century, according to Gregory of Tours, it was still used in isolated rural districts. In what is today Switzerland, Gallic was not finally eradicated until the arrival of the Alemanni in the fifth century. All this is certainly true. But after the first century AD these indigenous tongues, which were not supported by any linguistic nationalism, led an underground and constantly dwindling existence, whose historical significance was probably not very great.

Our problem is as follows: when a native population adopted Latin, they brought to it habits of vocabulary, pronunciation and even syntax – this was the classical action of the substratum. As a result, the Latin spoken in Gaul, the Latin spoken in Spain and the Latin spoken in Illyria and Dacia all began to develop distinct features. What exactly is the importance of these substrata and this divergence? Were the differences between the future Romance languages already appreciable as early as the second century AD? It is a difficult problem, and linguists are not unanimous as to its solution. On the contrary, completely opposed theories have been put forward. 'The division of the Romance languages began when the first province outside Italy was Romanised,' writes Gröber, 'and was completed as each new domain was conquered by Romance.' In France, Auguste Brun explains the opposition between the *langue d'oïl* and the *langue d'oc* as being essentially one between different substrata. In Spain, Ramón Menéndez Pidal attributes certain fundamental traits of Castilian to the influence of pre-Roman indigenous languages. Other linguists, on the contrary, emphasise more recent influences, and believe that towards the end of the second century AD, and in spite of regional differences, Latin had preserved its unity, and that its 'explosion' did not begin until later. This great controversy is nowhere near a conclusion, and the discussion of details leaves one with a somewhat ambiguous impression.

In the first place, the special features of Roman colonisation were certainly responsible for some differences which cannot be explained by the substratum. We may think, with Von Wartburg, that where Latin was introduced by members of the nobility it did not show the tendencies brought to other regions by plebeian colonists. The treatment of the final -*s* provides us with an example: it is dropped where the colonist belonged to the lower classes (rom. *doï*), and where peasant dialect triumphed (it. *due*), but it is preserved where the upper classes were responsible for Latinisation (fr. *deux*, sp. *dos*). It is much more dangerous to explain the difference between Portuguese and the Andalusian dialect (both conservative) and the more inventive Catalan, by an opposition between the urban and intellectual culture of the south and the more military and vulgar north-east, or to attribute the passage of *mb > m* and *l > ll* in Catalan to the effect of Oscan and Umbrian colonisation (the thesis supported by Menéndez Pidal, Meier and Gamillscheg). This is not impossible, but arguments derived from linguistic analysis remain debatable.

Something of the same sort occurs when an attempt is made to define in detail the influence of Celtic or Iberian substrata. The Celts were the chief victims of the battle for European expansion. As they spread from the east into Gaul, Brittany and Spain, they left Teutonic tribes living on the Rhine, and in Italy they were stopped by the Romans. Afterwards they were swamped by Germans and Italians in every part of the continent, and it was only in the British Isles that they were able to keep their independence. Tacitus assures us that Gallic and the Brythonic language of Brittany were very much alike. In opposition to the prevalent theory (Joseph Loth, Georges Dottin) that modern Breton was reintroduced after the fifth century AD, by islanders who took refuge in a completely Romanised Armorica, the Abbé Falc'hun has maintained that Gallic probably continued to exist in Armorica, and that Breton is its modern form. Leaving that apart, it must be admitted that very little is known about the Gallic language, so complete was its elimination. To reconstruct some of its features, linguists have had recourse mainly to toponymy (to go by its place-names, France is still partly a Celtic country) or all too rare inscriptions, or finally to comparing old French words, whose origin is neither Latin nor Germanic, with similar words preserved in the Celtic languages that are still spoken today. Von Wartburg succeeded in collecting about a hundred and eighty Celtic words that had passed into the Latin of Gaul. They were words for domestic or intimate use, such as *bertium (fr. berceau, prov. and cat. bres, port. berço), which triumphed over the Latin cuna. The French vocabulary of carpentry is still rich in terms of Gallic origin. Pierre, sable, mont, vallée are Latin words, because they represent very general topographic notions; but caillou, galet and boue, which translate a closer contact with the earth, are Gallic.

Did the inhabitants of Gaul pronounce Latin in a distinctive way? Recent research has tended to give less weight to the phonetic influence of the substratum, which was firmly believed in not long ago. But should it be altogether denied? The chief problem is the origin of the ü whose pronunciation gives many people who are not French such trouble; the development of the sound u (ou) towards the ü of modern French seems to correspond broadly with the Celtic zone (including northern Italy and parts of Portugal), and we also find in Celtic a frequent alternation between the sounds i and u. But the intermediate sound ü is not in evidence in Celtic, although it is found in German. We are left therefore with nothing but probabilities. A Latin of Gaul must have existed, but how much influence the Celtic substratum had on its special characteristics remains uncertain.

Let us move to the Iberian peninsula; here we do not even know what language or languages were spoken by the tribes conquered by the Romans. The standard reply used to be: in the east, Iberian (affirmed by Von Humboldt in 1821 to be identical with Basque), in the west, Celtic, and between the two, various mixtures which could be called 'Celtiberian'. But the identification of Basque with Iberian has been vigorously challenged, as has the importance of Celtic infiltration. More recently, Gerhard Rohlfs came to the conclusion, based on toponymy and the suffixes it made use of, that two populations must have existed: one race using the suffix -ossu, traces of which are found particularly in Gascony and Aragon, whose language may have been close to Basque; and another with the suffix *-oius* in Catalonia, possibly a branch of the Ligurians.

Whatever the precise nature of this substratum may have been, its influence on the vocabulary was undoubtedly slight. In phonology, the chief controversy concerns the evolution of the Latin initial *F* into the Castilian *H* (*filiam > hija*, cf. *hilha* in the Gascon dialect). Menéndez Pidal and Von Wartburg explain this by the influence of an indigenous population that did not possess this initial *f*, and transferred its phonetic habits to Latin. This theory is not impossible; though it runs contrary to several facts. First of all, a similar evolution is found in other countries; one could even say that it corresponds to a natural tendency of spoken Latin. Again, the Basques themselves, in their earliest borrowings from Latin, did not replace the initial *f* with *h*, but with a bilabial: thus *festa* became *besta, pesta*.

This whole discussion leaves us therefore with a somewhat disappointing impression. Spreading from little Latium throughout the Roman world, Latin cannot have remained the same everywhere. It naturally had to adopt different characteristics in every country, and enrich its vocabulary with local terms and habits of pronunciation; the morphological evolution of spoken Latin must have followed different lines from one place to the next. There was the Latin of Gaul (perhaps even several), the Latin of Spain, etc. But it remains extremely difficult to assess the contribution of the populations subjected to this evolution. It is just as difficult to date it exactly. Did the divergence between the Romance languages happen before or after the crisis of the third century? Linguists will go on answering this question in different ways according to their own inclinations.

Origins of the Germanic languages

Let us return to the first and second centuries AD. The European traveller who crossed the frontiers of *Romania* would meet with many different races, some Celtic, some perhaps pre-Indo-European: but among them the race we call Germanic would increasingly predominate. They did not adopt the name themselves, it was given them by Greek (Poséidonios) or Latin historians (Caesar, Tacitus); nor was the word applied to the Goths and Scandinavians, whom we now consider as among them. At all events the tribes concerned knew very little about each other, and cannot have had a strong or complete enough sense of their common origins to give rise to a comprehensive name.

We have good and purely linguistic reasons, however, for thinking that the name 'Germans' corresponded to a human reality. The Germanic races were those who spoke one of the languages belonging to one definite and distinctive branch of Indo-European. Just as the Romance languages all hark back to a proto-Romance which is also known as spoken Latin, so do the Germanic languages derive from a common stem we call 'proto-Germanic' (*Urgermanisch*). But we have no direct evidence of this mother tongue.

These Germanic races were in fact very slow to learn to write, although we cannot be quite sure that the oldest preserved written evidence was contemporary with the introduction of writing among them. We must wait until the fourth century AD for an important text: Ulfilas's Bible. Born about 311, the son of a Goth and a Cappadocian prisoner, Ulfilas received a solid Christian education; he spoke and wrote Latin and Greek. While on a mission to Constantinople, he was promoted to a bishopric. In order to spread Christianity among the Goths, probably to the north of the lower Danube, he decided to translate the Bible. It was an arduous task, for he had to invent an alphabet and a whole vocabulary. Part of this work has come down to us and is a document of unique value for our knowledge of proto-Germanic. However, it only acquaints us, and that at a late date, with a single branch, Gothic, which has since disappeared. Furthermore it is sacred

writing, strongly influenced by Greek and certainly very different from familiar language. And it has been handed down to
us in a not very satisfactory condition: we have only a few
fragments, and those in the form of a copy made in the fifth or
sixth century, perhaps in the region of Brescia, some of the
Goths having settled in Italy. This is the *Codex Argenteus*, a
beautiful parchment written in silver and gold ink on a purple
ground; it was found in the sixteenth century in the monastery
of Werden (near Cologne) and is now preserved at Uppsala,
close to the original home of the Goths. It is not impossible
that the language was deliberately modernised by copyists,
quite apart from possible carelessness on their part.

In spite of all these difficulties, the case of the Goths is much
the most rewarding. We have to wait until the seventh and
eighth centuries for manuscripts in early High German and
old English, and until the ninth for early Saxon. Of course,
from the third century onwards, we possess weapons and jewels
with runic inscriptions: but these are to some extent magic
formulae, mysterious even to the populations for whom they
were intended.

Circumstances obliged the Romans to take an interest in
these races, and led them to reproduce some of their words,
particularly their names, in writing. Insofar as the authors had
a good ear and were anxious to transcribe these vocables
exactly, this evidence cannot be completely disregarded.

By such imperfect means as these we can gain access to the
Germanic languages, though not to proto-Germanic. They do
however provide landmarks to guide us in our attempt to reach
back to proto-Germanic by comparing the grammars of the
Germanic languages – a task whose difficulty can best be
illustrated by an example. Words found in the whole body of
Germanic languages may come from a common stem. Thus the
Gothic *stains*, the o. icel. *steinn*, the o. eng. *stan*, the o. s. *sten*,
the o. h. ger. *stein* take us back to a stem meaning 'stone'. Its
termination in the nominative singular is found by examining

the runic Norse form (*stainar*) and early borrowings by Finnish from Germanic (such as the word *Kuningas*). From all this, the proto-ger. **stainaz* can be deduced, corresponding to an Indo-European termination *-os*.

Such operations shed but a faint light on proto-Germanic. Enough to prompt historians to ask themselves the questions: where and when was this common language spoken? When and how did the collective migrations occur which led to its 'explosion'? Here again, our documentation is extremely meagre. We are reduced to consulting the writings of Latin historians and geographers, as well as the traditions handed down by these peoples themselves and collected by later writers. Toponymy and archaeology furnish us with means of testing these sometimes ill-informed, sometimes legendary data. Does a relationship exist between the toponyms found in two regions, or the roughly dated results of archaeological excavations? Do these relationships correspond to some linguistic kinship? Such lines of research can obviously only lead to hypothetical conclusions.

Within such limits, it is now more or less accepted that proto-Germanic must have been the language spoken in the Scandinavian peninsula, Denmark, and the northern Germany of today at a period that some authorities place in about the first century BC, and others in the third and fourth centuries BC. According to which view is taken, it is thought to have begun to spread either during the lifetime of Jesus Christ or in the second and third centuries BC.

It is possible to reconstruct certain phonetic, morphologic and even syntactic features of this common language:

1 Under the first heading, we notice the absence of certain vocalic sounds, such as ŏ: thus the ind. eur. **okto*, which remains *octo* in Latin, becomes *ahtau* in got. (ger. *acht*). But the essential characteristic is what has been called Germanic consonantal mutation, or first mutation, in opposition to a

second and later one which was only to affect certain Germanic dialects. Let us take a few examples: Latin has *decem*, got. *taihun*, whence modern English *ten* (but modern German, affected by the second mutation, has *zehn*). The voiced occlusive *d* becomes an unvoiced *t*. In the same way, to the Latin word *pecu* corresponds the English *fee*, and German *Vieh*: the unvoiced occlusive *p* has developed into the spirant *f*. These broad changes affect nearly all occlusives and give the language a truly new aspect. Finally, an intensive accent is placed on the first syllable, stressing it strongly, while the other syllables grow weaker or even tend to disappear. This is how the Latin Colonia later became transformed into the German Köln, whereas it is preserved in the French form Cologne.

2 The other aspects can be dealt with more briefly, since although they are just as interesting to linguists they do not make such an obvious contribution to the special physiognomy of the language. Proto-Germanic makes a fairly common, though not universal use of vocalic alteration. Thus it opposes the strong conjugations of verbs, based on this alternation according to an Indo-European type (got. *steigan*, *staig*, *stigans*: to climb), to the weak conjugations, which merely add a suffix (as in the preterite, got. *nasi-da*, I have saved, o. h. ger. *nerita*, mod. ger. *nährte*). In the same way there are strong and weak declensions for nouns and adjectives. There was a special declension for adjectives in proto-Germanic. But in other respects its morphology is a great deal simpler than that of Indo-European. The number of forms is definitely smaller both for conjugations and declensions.

3 Finally, the syntax is obviously the most difficult aspect to reconstruct. We will confine ourselves to noting that proto-Germanic, like Latin, seems to have used neither subjective personal pronouns nor articles. The article appears in

Gothic alone, and in a purely facultative manner, probably under the influence of Greek. What is the explanation of the fact that the Germanic branch developed these original characteristics? How can we decide whether it evolved spontaneously among certain Indo-European tribes, or was the result of an ethnic mixture, occurring when these tribes gradually merged with pre-Indo-European populations, whose substratum must have influenced their language? However attractive these speculations may appear, they must necessarily be treated as hypotheses.

It would seem as if we were on more solid ground when we come to the problem of the ramifications of proto-Germanic, that is to say the classification of the Germanic languages derived from it. The classical and traditional division into three areas is based on the evolution of such words as the proto-Germanic *dala-z (valley).

Firstly we have an oriental area, known only through the got. *dals*. All its branches have disappeared, and Gothic is the only language known to have left traces. The nordic area was that of *dalr*: it corresponds to Scandinavian, Norwegian, Swedish and Icelandic. The western area was that of *dal*, but it was afterwards fragmented: only Low German, and later Dutch, kept *dal*, which developed into *tal* in High German, *del* in Frisian, *dael* in old English.

This richness of western articulation is what makes classification most difficult. Authors like Maurer, and more recently Schwarz, have suggested different schemas. Schwarz contrasts the conservative Germans from the north (Scandinavians, Goths), whose language was rather close to proto-Germanic, with the Germans of the south, who made contact with indigenous populations and even the Roman world, and were much more given to innovation. He sees a Germanic language of the North Sea slowly evolving between them. This would have stretched from Jutland to the mouth of the Rhine, and would only have adopted some of the innovations from the south. In the fifth century AD, the departure of the Angles and Saxons for Britain would have broken this unity. Other schemas have been worked out, and their diversity underlines the complexity of the problem.

The two branches that chiefly concern us here were thus detached from the Indo-European stem, and their development seems to have followed very different lines. The Italic races had been established in Italy at least from the sixth century BC, and one of them had been astonishingly successful: the Latins unified Italy, and made themselves masters of the whole of western Europe and the Mediterranean. They produced a very abundant literature, and if their daily conversation differed somewhat from it, it is possible to form a relatively precise idea of it. One branch had developed, stifling the others. But the very expansion of the Latin language produced a diversification whence came the Romance languages. Thus in the south we find an only child but an extraordinarily vigorous and prolific one, who learned to write early and can be well known thereby.

The Germanic people remained vagrants for much longer, and took several centuries more to acquire the art of writing, from seven to ten or eleven as the case might be! Many of them disappeared, but only by merging with the Italic family. None dominated his brothers; no Germanic language stifled the rest. In the north then, we have a large family, slow to learn to write, and much less well known. We shall find the characteristics again, on more than one occasion.

WE ALL KNOW the ancient sophism: Here is a man with thick hair. His hairs are removed one by one. The loss of one hair cannot make him bald. So in the end he has not a single hair left on his head, yet no one has ever called him bald. The same problem, which consists in introducing discontinuity into a continuous series, recurs in our present study. During the first centuries of the Christian era, Latin was broadly speaking the general language of *Romania*. In the eleventh century the Romance languages were being spoken there, and the distinction between them and Latin had become conscious. Modern scholars have therefore wondered: when did people stop speaking Latin? Strictly speaking, the question does not admit of a reply. Uninitiated common sense hopes to be given one, nevertheless.

In the Germanic world similar developments were taking place. Separate languages were formed, derived from the common Germanic stem. The first monuments to the English and German languages can be dated during the seventh and eighth century. This half-millennium was thus of essential importance for the whole of Europe.

Problems of method

In answer to the question: during which three years of his life does a man learn most? the most reasonable reply is probably the first three. Yet these are precisely the ones that a psychologist has most difficulty in penetrating. We are up against an analogous difficulty here. Of course our documentation for the Romance languages is relatively good, thanks to the numerous texts in existence. But very delicate problems are raised as soon as we try to utilise them.

All these texts are in fact written in Latin. In following their chronological development, changes are observable between one text and the next. But the texts of the seventh and eighth centuries are still in Latin, although we are now reaching the period when contemporaries thought it necessary to give a different name to the spoken language. As late as the fifth century, and probably later, one can detect the passage of written to oral language as a change of style. In about 800 it became a change of language. Of these two divergent paths, only one is directly made known to us by the texts. We hardly possess any direct evidence of the spoken language. Herein lies our difficulty.

Nevertheless, we can ask ourselves whether something of the spoken language was not reflected in writing. The answer is likely to vary according to the nature of the texts. It will be pessimistic in the case of literary writing, whether it is a question of a 'precious' writer like Sidonius Apollinaris (died about 485), or a historian like Gregory of Tours (538–94), whose protestations of ignorance should not mislead us: they merely serve to draw attention to the excellence of his style! A more encouraging reply is possible in the case of deliberately popular writing, intended to be understood by the more or less illiterate masses: sermons, accounts of pilgrimages or the lives of saints. Probably even fewer literary pretensions can be attributed to legal texts: summaries of Barbarian laws, royal charters, acts in Council, formularies for the use of drafters of acts. But the very existence of these formularies reminds us that the respect for models and tradition was a powerful factor tending to archaism in that department of life.

Finally it is possible to compare these texts with the evidence gained from toponymy. Throughout the centuries place-names have been created, in greater or less numbers according to the region. Such quantitative data are themselves indicative of the importance of a given 'Barbarian' settlement. And the physiognomy of the vocables used in forming these place-names will very probably reveal the real words that go to make them up, and even their pronunciation.

Whatever texts may be under consideration, problems of transmission arise. With very few exceptions, literary texts are known to us through more recent copies: has the scribe altered them slightly, either from carelessness or so as to adapt them to the taste of the day? A good many legal texts are fakes, manufactured at a later date: this is true of about half the charters that claim to date from the Merovingian epoch. As for place-names, one must always look for their oldest forms. Thus the material has to be subjected to preliminary 'treatment' by scholars, and this demands great care, and prudence in drawing conclusions.

Even so, not all the changes in a spoken language were equally likely to be reflected in the same text. The novelty of some of them must have aroused the scribe's interest and provoked his reticence. We have already mentioned the early dropping of the final *m*: it was easy for a scribe to write *porta* instead of *portam*, because after all *porta* was a well-known Latin form; but *septe* corresponded to nothing he knew, so the scribe went on writing *septem*. Another example tells us even more:

In the Strasbourg Oaths we come across forms of the type *salvarai* for *salvare habeo*, in which the two elements of what was to become the French future tense were welded together. In the spoken language these forms must have existed much earlier. But as they were of a completely new type, Latin texts provide no examples that could help us fix the chronology of this development. Fredegarius happens to have proved for us that this unification had already been realised by the beginning of the seventh century. He made a play on words and wrote *daras* for *dare habes*, when alluding to the proper name *Daras*.[4]

A comparison between the grammars of the Romance languages teaches us a great deal about the nature of their divergence from the common stem, as a few examples will show:

In opposition to *capra* in Italian, and *capră* in Romanian, we have *cabra* in Spanish and *cabra* in Occitan, showing the voicing of the labial. In French the *b* afterwards became the labiodental *v*: *chèvre*.

The present indicative of the verb *aller* in French reveals a curious mixture of forms derived from *ire* in Latin, *andare* in vulg. lat., and a rather mysterious *alare*:

SP.	PORT.	OCC.	FR.	IT.
voy	*vou*	*vau, vauc*	*vais* (o. fr. *vois*)	*vado, vo*
vas	*vais*	*vas*	*vas* (o. fr. *vais*)	*vai*
va	*vai*	*va, vai*	*va* (o. fr. *vait*)	*va*
vamos	*imos*	*anam*	*allons*	*andiamo*
vais	*ides, is*	*anatz*	*allez*	*andate*
van	*vam*	*van*	*vont*	*vanno*

Lastly, Karl Baldinger has collected together the features characteristic of the divergent development of the Iberian languages in the following sentence:

Sp.: *El ocho de enero, el hijo ciego llegò a la huerta con un cesto lleno de piedras y una paloma de color blanco.*

Cat.: *El vuit de gener, el fill cec arribà a l'horta amb un cistell ple de pedres i una coloma de color blanc.*

Port.: *No dia oito de janeiro, o filho cego chegou à horta com um cesto cheio de pedras e uma pômba de côr branco.*

(On 8 January, the blind son arrived at the garden with a basket full of stones and a white dove.)

Such comparisons as these enable us to retrace the history of each spoken language, and describe and qualify its divergence from Latin. But they do not in themselves help us to date them.

The methods suggested here may be supplemented to a certain extent by establishing what is known as the 'relative chronology' of changes. This was first done for phonetic changes by Georges Straka. He started from the idea that such changes, from Latin to a Romance language, could not happen in a random order. Take the transition from the lat. *caru(m)* to fr. *chier* (mod. *cher*): the *a* has been lengthened and then converted into the diphthong *ie*; but the palatisation of *c* into *tch* must certainly have happened earlier, for it would not have taken place had the consonant preceded the diphthong *ie*. Thus a chain is constructed, wherein changes can be dated relatively to each other. How can we pass from this relative chronology to an absolute one? First, it is an accepted fact that a change needs at least a generation, or thirty years, to become generally accepted; so that when two changes are separated by four others, we can assume that a period of from a hundred and twenty to a hundred and fifty years intervened between them.

Landmarks must also be looked for: if the study of Latin texts enables us to prove that a certain change took place at the end of the fifth century, the whole chain can almost certainly be placed within that time. Straka maintains that a similar task can be carried out for morphological and syntactic changes.

However, even though considerable work has already been done, there is still room for a great deal more. And a hypothetical element will probably always remain in the conclusions reached by linguists.

Latin and Christianity

The 'great invasions', which may reasonably be taken as the most important events between the third and tenth centuries, were preceded by another change, whose effects they increased. Our first question should be: what did Christianity contribute to Latin?

At first the religion of a tiny minority, Christianity slowly became that of the entire Roman world. The death of Christ, between the years 28 and 30, was followed by a period when the first oriental Christian communities increased and divided to form new communities. Very soon Christianity appeared in Rome, where it was distinguished from the religion of the Jews and made illegal. In 64, the burning of Rome under Nero was followed by the execution of many Christians. By that time Paul had established numerous churches in the Hellenistic world. There were about thirty in the Roman Empire at the beginning of the second century. By about 180, Christianity had reached Gaul, Spain and North Africa. In 325, delegates of these churches met at the Council of Nicaea to settle the terminology of dogma. After surviving persecution, the Christian Church finally triumphed. In 380, an edict of Theodosius I imposed the Nicaean Creed. But paganism had not vanished.

From the very start, Christianity introduced a whole body of new ideas, connected with dogma and theology, morality and the Christian outlook, as well as with the organisation of the Church and religious worship. These concepts, these feelings, these institutions, these things all had to be referred to. As Christianity came to Rome from the East, its arrival meant fresh borrowings from Greek: borrowings that were at first scholarly but later became subjected to popularisation among communities largely recruited from the humbler ranks of society. The combination of these factors must have led to different developments.

Thus the leader of a Christian community was called *episcopus*: this word produced the o. fr. *evesque*, where the maintenance of the group *sc* reveals a scholarly evolution (popular evolution would probably have given **evesve*); in sp. *obispo* seems more popular, except for the preservation of the vowel *i*; the it. *vescovo*, however, is an entirely popular formation. Notice, by the way, that ger. was to adopt *Bischof*, eng. *bishop*, etc. . . . Another example, the word *basilica*, for the religious edifice, soon disappeared (except in the East, where it was perpetualised in the rom. *biserică*), and was supplanted by *ecclesia*: here the evolution is always popular, towards the it. *chiesa*, Sardinian *keya*, cat. *esglesia*, sp. *iglesia*, port. *igreja*, occ. *glieisa*, fr. *église*. On the other hand Germanic adopted a word formed from the Greek, which produced ger. *Kirche*, eng. *church*, sc. *kirk*, and Dutch *kerk*.

Some of these specifically Christian words passed out of the purely religious domain. For instance we notice in the Gospels the great number of 'parables' used by Christ: 'The kingdom of Heaven', he declared, 'is like to a mustard-seed.' These comparisons (for this is the exact significance of the word *parabola*, adopted by Latin) were considered so characteristic that the word *parabola* came to mean the word of God. It was afterwards applied to preaching, as an extension of the divine utterance. Finally, it supplanted the lat. *loqui* and acquired the very general meaning we find in the it. *parlare*, cat. *parlar*, occ. *paraular* and fr. *parler*. However, the more conservative Spanish and Portuguese kept to the lat. *fabulari*, from which *hablar* and *falar* were derived.

No less interesting to linguists are what might be called 'indirect Christianisms'. These are terms or expressions found in the work of Christian authors alone (such as the adverbs *subsequenter*, *veraciter*, and verbs in -*ficare*: *vivificare*, *honorificare* etc), which, however, 'are not naturally associated with Christianity'.[5] Many of these are first found in Tertullian. Born at Carthage between 150 and 155, of good family, he was first destined for a legal career. But after a thorough education he became a Christian. He was the founder of Christian literature in the Latin language. But he does not seem to have been personally responsible for these expressions; they were created in the heart of those Christian communities that existed for many years like small closed and secret worlds, threatened from without. Some of them savour a little of the emphasis naturally given by religious exaltations and awareness of danger. This 'sectarian language' gradually developed until it became a truly literary language. Later on, when Christianity had triumphed over persecution, had become the official religion and spread throughout the Empire, a sort of Christian language came into existence, determined by its use of strictly Christian terms, but also by all these linguistic factors. And just as, during the progressive break-up of the Empire, religion and the Church were the principal factors tending towards unity, so this Christian Latin was able to preserve some degree of coherence. Certain writers, such as H. F. Muller, have spoken (probably not without exaggeration) of a sort of 'pre-Romance *koinè*'.

Another effect of Christianity was to recommend simplicity in the spoken language as in the written language. It was a question here of a practical rule: if Christian preachers wanted to be understood by the often uneducated masses they wished to convert, they must speak to them as simply as possible. But there was more involved, and we must understand what Christians meant by *sermo humilis*. Before their time, this expression normally indicated a low, ordinary style, such as Cicero would have used in a lawsuit or to deal with money matters. But surely the qualification *humilis* (or 'close to the soil', *humus*), was applicable to the life led by Christ among men, and his sufferings? His was a voluntary humiliation, glorified by the Evangelists and St Paul, and set up as an example to Christians. The Bible itself – and its subsequent Latin translation – was written in a very simple style. So were the earliest Christian writings, so much so that cultured pagans thought them childish and vulgar. But the Christians declared that they possessed a new and deeper sublimity, needing proper understanding.

Christianity gave language a new social function. Henceforth it must be used to convince and move the masses, and so to create a sort of popular rhetoric. Its deliberate humility was enhanced by the sublimity it helped to reveal, and at the same time it was a necessary condition of this revelation.

Most Christian authors continued to write along these lines throughout the centuries, at least when their words were destined to reach a large public. During the third century, an abundance of Christian literature was written. Its syntax was particularly notable in that it had abandoned the complicated structure of classical Latin: a few simple prepositions (such as *ad*, *de*, *in* and *pro*) were systematically used to link words together; phrases were simply juxtaposed. Of course all these tendencies already existed in spoken Latin. What was new was their promotion to literary language, and their function of dealing with any subject, however noble.

The Fathers of the Church, such as St Jerome and St Augustine, deliberately adopted this line. It was the latter who wrote: '*Melius est reprehendant nos grammatici quam non intelligant populi*'. (It is better for our grammarians to reproach us than for the masses not to understand.) In the sixth century, St Cesarius of Arles was to insist vigorously on the necessity for a 'simple and plain' language. In the meantime perhaps the masterpiece of this genre was *A Pilgrimage to the Holy Places*, most often attributed to a Spanish nun called Egeria, living in the early fifth century – a very simple work, but fresh in outlook and delightfully lively (see page 66).

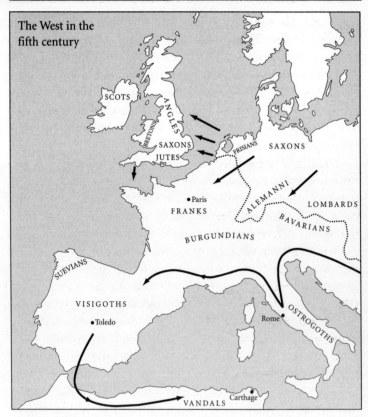

The West in the fifth century

SCOTS
ANGLES
BRETONS
SAXONS
JUTES
FRISIANS
SAXONS
•Paris
FRANKS
ALEMANNI
LOMBARDS
BAVARIANS
BURGUNDIANS
SUEVIANS
VISIGOTHS
•Toledo
Rome•
OSTROGOTHS
VANDALS
Carthage•

However, when Egeria was writing, *Romania* had already been invaded.

The effect of the invasions

A description of the invasions would not be in place here: it is to be found in several excellent works. We will only emphasise a few points. These 'invasions' were not new phenomena: Rome had always had to defend herself against them. During the two first centuries of the Christian era pressure from other races had been contained. In the middle of the third century, the Roman *limes* (equivalent to the Great Wall of China) was

breached, and the 'Barbarians' spread throughout *Romania*.
Certain particularly exposed territories were abandoned: the
Agri Decumates in the south-west corner of Germania, and
Dacia north of the lower Danube. This was the price of
reconstructing the Rhine-Danube frontier. However, the
infiltration of 'Barbarians' into the Empire continued, and
Roman armies were partly recruited from among them. What
was new at the beginning of the fifth century was that the
breach opened in the *limes* had become definitive and was never
again to be filled up.

It was during the night of 31 December 406, that the Rhine
was crossed by peoples who had appeared several centuries
earlier in the Scandinavian regions: Vandals, Alans, Suevians
and Burgundians. This break-through was facilitated by the
fact that the Empire had to concentrate its defences in Italy
against another Germanic race from the East, the Visigoths,
although without being able to prevent them taking Rome and
pillaging it in 410. The races invading *Romania* gradually
established themselves: after crossing Gaul and remaining in
Spain for a time, the Vandals founded a kingdom in north
Africa; the others stopped on the way, the Burgundians in
Gaul, the Suevians in Spain. The Visigoths intended at first to
go to north Africa, but instead they invaded south-west Gaul
and spread into Spain. This first wave was completed by the
establishment of the Ostrogoths, another branch of the Goths,
in Italy in 489.

A second wave was created nearer home by the slow expansion of the races that had settled in Germany. The more or less
homogeneous group known as the Franks was united by Clovis
(481–511) and established itself as far as the Loire, before
embarking on war with the Burgundians, Alemanni and
Visigoths. Deprived of most of their territory in Gaul (except
what was to become lower Languedoc), the latter founded the
kingdom of Toledo in Spain. Absorbing the Alemanni from
the upper Rhine and the Bavarians from southern Germania,

the successors of Clovis – and of his legendary ancestor Merovaeus, who gave them their name of Merovingians – finally formed a powerful state, which reached its apogee in about 560.

At this time Justinian's attempt at reconquest had ruined the Vandal State in north Africa and afterwards the Ostrogoth State in Italy, and snatched back some of the Visigoths' territory in Spain. But the results were mainly negative, and opened the way to more invaders, the Lombards in Italy (568) and the Arabs in Africa and Spain. By his inability to attack the Frankish State he helped construct its future importance.

The picture is completed by several migrations by sea. Angles, Saxons and Jutes, who had settled in and near present-day Jutland, began to ravage the coasts from Scotland to the Gironde. They finally founded several kingdoms in Britain, which had been evacuated by the Roman legions in 407, after the crossing of the Rhine. The Britons were driven westwards into Wales and Cornwall; but there were some who took refuge in Armorica.

It was very much later that the Arabs conquered north Africa, and diverted the warlike zeal of its inhabitants, the Berbers, to Spain. They landed near Gibraltar in 711 and conquered nearly the whole peninsula within a few years. They even made some inroads into Gaul, but were finally driven back. In about 800, the Franks helped the inhabitants of what is now northern Catalonia to free themselves from the Moors. But for more than two centuries after this, most of Spain enjoyed a prosperous material and intellectual life under Moorish rule.

Apart from these Moors, the migrant races, even when their ethnic origins differed, all spoke Germanic languages. None of them was very numerous, they remained mere minorities in the midst of more or less Romanised indigenous populations. But these minorities exercised power by right of conquest, took part in the administration, and avoided being absorbed by remaining in groups. They did not show any systematic hostility to Latin culture on the whole. There were also regions where the human contribution resulting from the invasions was much more important: the Franks in northern Gaul (particularly north of the Somme), and the Angles and Saxons in Britain (where they were reinforced by a continuous stream of immigrants) may even have made up a majority of the population. Fusion took place everywhere, and community of religion was not unconnected with this fact.

This movement continued well on into the sixth century, when the Lombards arrived in Italy. Meantime the Slavs were gradually spreading into eastern Europe, and, until the beginning of the seventh century, Bretons expelled from the British Isles by the expansion of the Angles and Saxons sought refuge in Armorica. To this ethnic upheaval might be added the Moorish conquest at the beginning of the eighth century, which put almost the whole of the Iberian peninsula under the domination of a Semitic race. It is interesting to contemplate all these events together, and use the differences between them for a fruitful comparative study of their linguistic consequences.

We are at once struck by the modification of the linguistic map at the expense of Latin, although episodes in the nature of revivals did occur. Pre-Roman spoken languages regained their influence in regions that had been only feebly Romanised. This was the case with Basque, which covered a larger linguistic area than it does nowadays. The position of Armorica is more debatable: until recently linguists believed that this region had been fully Romanised, and that Breton was only reintroduced in the seventh and eighth centuries by refugees from the British Isles; but the Abbé Falc'hun maintains that their appearance only strengthened the Celtic revival, which had already been stimulated by the decline of Roman domination.

In the Iberian peninsula under Moorish rule, the language derived from Latin was still used but played a subsidiary part:

for centuries to come Arabic would be the language of culture, used by the more civilised 'Mozarabic' Christians.

In every other case the losses of Latin benefited the Germanic or Slavonic languages. In the British Isles, abandoned by the Roman legions in 407, the Angles and Saxons found Breton mixed with Latinisms a century later: for this reason Anglo-Saxon was only slightly influenced by Latin (and that at a late date, connected with their conversion to Christianity); as for Breton, it borrowed almost nothing from this language – a revealing indication of the bitter opposition between the two.

The linguistic frontier on the continent still remained – a sort of volcanic zone, which produced (and still produces) so many eruptions. The map shows clearly enough what serious losses Latinity had suffered. But it does not take into account anomalies such as those we shall summarise here:

1 In the East, it is surprising to find hardly any traces of Latin in that *Illyricum* so long occupied by Rome, now part of Yugoslavia. It is even more surprising that such traces do exist in Dacia, where the Romans ventured north of the Danube, only to evacuate it as early as 271. Did Italian colonists take refuge in the Carpathians or Transylvania, and descend afterwards into the plains of the Danube? Or did they cross the Danube southwards, to regain their old home at a later date? At all events, they were vigorous enough to endow present-day Romania with a language which has remained a Romance language and was noticed as such by linguists at the end of the sixteenth century, in spite of the Slavonic locutions that penetrated it.

2 It was probably in the central sector, corresponding to the occupation by the Bavarians and Alemanni, that the loss of ground by the Latin language was most noticeable. In Bavaria south of the Danube we see a total collapse of *Romania*. The Germanic onslaughts continued for a long time: they crossed

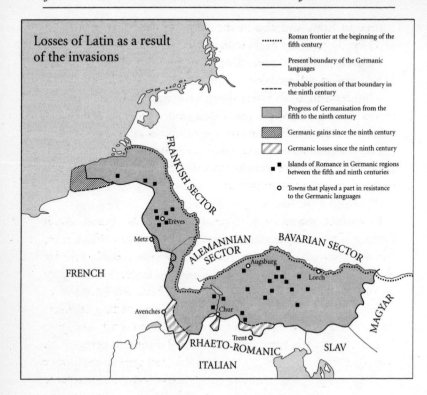

Losses of Latin as a result of the invasions

.... Roman frontier at the beginning of the fifth century

———— Present boundary of the Germanic languages

– – – – Probable position of that boundary in the ninth century

▨ Progress of Germanisation from the fifth to the ninth century

▨ Germanic gains since the ninth century

▨ Germanic losses since the ninth century

■ Islands of Romance in Germanic regions between the fifth and ninth centuries

○ Towns that played a part in resistance to the Germanic languages

FRANKISH SECTOR

Trèves

Metz

ALEMANNIAN SECTOR

BAVARIAN SECTOR

Augsburg

Lorch

FRENCH

MAGYAR

Avenches

Chur

Trent

RHAETO-ROMANIC

SLAV

ITALIAN

the Brenner in the seventh century and invaded the upper Adige in the eighth. In Switzerland, pressure by the Alemanni was no less vigorous: at first, the Latin language resisted in some towns, like Chur, but it was afterwards locked away in the high valleys of the Grisons and Engadine. Farther west, where the advance of the Alemanni was halted by the Merovingians, the linguistic boundary was established in the Vosges, slightly to the east of the highest range.

3 The Frankish sector has perhaps been the subject of the most diverse hypotheses. One gets a definite impression that there were considerable fluctuations in the linguistic frontier until the thirteenth century. Islets of Romance subsisted for a long

time in Eifel, and also in the valley of the Moselle, around Trier. Toponymy bears witness to this: thus the place-name *Tabernae*, which normally develops into *Zabern* (today *Saverne*) in a Germanic country, has become *Tawern* in the neighbourhood of Trier, showing a region where Romance was long preserved, but which was finally Germanised. Conversely, the Boulonnais was occupied by Saxons (giving many place-names in -*tun*: such as Abinctun, cf. Abingdon), but their influence gave way to that of the Franks; between the ninth and thirteenth century this country was Romanised.

Important traces of Germanisation can be found much further afield. Linguists such as Gamillscheg and Wartburg, and the historian Petri have systematically observed them as far as the line Abbeville – Versailles – Nancy, beyond which they become much fewer. Example: Rebais en Brie, recorded in 635 under the form *Resbacis*, and constructed according to Germanic rules on the Frankish word *baki* (stream); compare Rossbach. This is the zone of maximal Frankish settlement. These authors have suggested that this vast region must have been thoroughly Germanised, that bilingualism persisted there until the ninth century, and that its linguistic reconquest by Romance happened later.

This argument does not carry absolute conviction. It is quite possible that Frankish nuclei persisted for a certain time, in a more or less unstable state, without it being accurate to speak of bilingualism. At any rate, whether the spread of Frankish was stopped at the present frontier between Flemish and Walloon in Belgium, or whether that frontier resulted from a later victory for Romance, its rectilinear outline, impossible to reduce to terms of any ancient political frontier, still fascinates both linguists and historians.

Everywhere else Latin imposed itself upon the invaders. But the 'invasions' did not merely alter the linguistic map of Europe. They also emphasised the evolution that had been going on within *Romania* since before the fifth century, namely the divergence of regional forms of spoken Latin, and the development of features that were to remain common to the Romance languages.

The most direct influence of the 'invasions' and the easiest to detect, was their effect as superstrata. While learning and adopting the Latin language – a development undoubtedly favoured by numerous mixed marriages – the invaders introduced terms from their own language, as well as phonetic, morphological and even syntactic habits. The penetration of the 'Barbarian' vocabulary is the least debatable. But the modification of pronunciation is almost beyond doubt also: a rather sinister monarch, but one who prided himself on his learning, the Merovingian king Chilperic (561–84), was so conscious of the inadequacy of the Latin alphabet to translate the sounds of the Latin he heard spoken around him, that he suggested adding some characters, corresponding in particular with the spirant *th*. The contribution of the superstratum varied from one region to another: these differences are explained by very diverse factors, the respective number of invaders and indigenous inhabitants, the type of settlement the former adopted, the human relationships developing between the two, and their mentalities.

Not only did the contribution of each race have its own distinctive characteristics, but the nature and proportion of the mixture constituted a further element of divergence. Let us briefly consider the chief cases.

The case of Italy is particularly complex. For here several superstrata were superimposed, the Ostrogoths, the Lombards and even the Franks after the end of the eighth century, so that it is difficult to make out what part each played. Moreover, Italian unity is a recent event, dialects have preserved a vigorous life for a very long time, and a question of principle arises: should the Barbarian contributions be assessed from Italian or from the dialects? At all events the Ostrogothic contribution was obviously slight: about seventy words, none of which refers to administration or the army. This was not only because the Ostrogoths were quite soon eliminated (or nearly) by Justinian's reconquests, but also because their sovereigns had carefully kept them apart from the rest of the population.

Let us therefore turn to the contribution of the Lombards. About 280 words of Lombard origin have been absorbed into Italian, and more still into Italian dialects. Curiously enough, hardly any of these refer either to the administration or the army: it is natural to suppose that this was not the case at first, but that the final triumph of the Franks helped eliminate these Lombard vocables. The words adopted belong to the vocabulary of daily life, and relate to the parts of the body (*strozza*-throat, *schiena*-back, *zazzera*-long hair!), or to architecture (*scuro*-shutter, *stamberga*-hut). There is also a series of adjectives with emotive meanings, to describe a man as cunning (*lesto*), or bad (*gramo*) etc. And we can attribute to Lombard influence certain phonetic phenomena, such as the evolution of intervocalic occlusives (*sapere* > pied. *saveye*), or the diphthongisation of the free tonic vowels (*piede* in opposition to *perde*; *nuovo* to *corpo*).

In fact the linguistic geography of Italy seems to have acquired a new look as a result of the Lombard settlement. This took place chiefly in the north, in an area roughly corresponding to the Lombard kingdom with its centre at Pavia; it is here that we find most of the place-names ending in *-engo*, or the place-name *Fara* (a word standing for a small band of Barbarians); it is here that dialects are spoken showing the strongest lexical and phonetic influence. This kingdom must therefore have covered part of the old zone of Celtic influence in Italy, bounded to the south by the Spezia-Rimini line. But part only, since it also included Tuscany. On the other hand the Lombard duchies of Spoleto and Benevento descended much further down the boot. A word like *schiena* (see above) occurs

Italo- and Rhaeto-Romance

Linguistic frontiers:
The Spezia–Rimini line was the southern
limit of the zone of Celtic influence.

again in the dialect of the Benevento region. Only Naples and the extreme south, which had remained under Byzantine rule, acquired nothing. So that Lombard influence did not strengthen the linguistic dualism to be found on both sides of the Spezia–Rimini line; on the contrary it diminished it, so avoiding an eventual break-up of Italian linguistic unity.

Things happened very differently in Gaul, where the action of the superstrata was to confirm and reinforce that of the substrata. Neither the Visigoths of the Aquitanian basin nor the Ostrogoths in Provence were very numerous; both were already sufficiently Romanised at the time of their settlement, and they quickly abandoned their languages and culture; the victory of the Franks finally reduced their influence even more, or made some of them decide to depart. The evolution of spoken languages peculiar to southern France was therefore very little affected. The situation seems to have been slightly different for the Burgundians, who had probably settled in larger numbers. Of course their lexical contribution remained fairly small, even to local dialects. Yet the map shows a rather disturbing coincidence between the zone of Burgundian settlement and the future area of Franco-Provençal, the intermediate spoken language between the south and the north.

It was in Frankish territory north of the Loire that a situation in fact developed whose originality historians do not fail to stress; an abundant Frankish population, the absence (since the beginning of the sixth century) of all political or religious barriers between Franks and Romans, the creation of a powerful and victorious state, becoming weaker in the seventh and eighth centuries but reinvigorated later by the Carolingians – everything combined to create a quite unique fusion. It is more or less true to say that its result, linguistically at least, was France: as early as the eighth century the word *Frantia* appeared against *Gallia* in a glossary, and the French owe their name to the Latinisation of the vocable *Frankisk*.

The lexical contribution of the Franks was considerable: about 520 words have passed into French – out of nearly 700, all of which did not survive. We will confine ourselves, like Gamillscheg, to a classification that seems illuminating. First we have a number of terms relating to the state and the administration: we may quote *sini-skalk > sénéchal* (senior servant, major-domo), *marh-skalk > maréchal* (stable-man), or again *al-ôd* (whole property) > *alodum* > alleu, and *feh-ôd* (movable property) > *feudum*, root transformed into *féodal*. It is the same with the vocabulary of war; terms which had been Latinised by the Franks themselves early on were adopted by the Gallo-Romans, because there were no Latin terms exactly corresponding to these institutions of a strongly Germanised state.

Other words belonging to the domains of agriculture, vegetation, the family or the emotions show what a long resistance the Franks put up to assimilation. The Latin word for beech, *fagus*, existed, and gave rise to the occ. *fau*, sp. *haya*, cat. *faig*, Basque *bago*, it. *faggio*, rom. *fag*: but it was the Frankish term *hestr* that prevailed. Similarly with *brut*, corresponding to the ger. *Braut*, eng. *bride*, which was to give the fr. *bru*. No emotion is more intimate than shame: in southern countries people went on expressing it by *verecundia*, whence came occ. *vergonha*, cat. *vergonya*, sp. *verguenza* and it. *vergogna*; but the French word *honte* comes from the Frankish *haunitha*. The only domains that remained almost intact were those of commerce and craftsmanship, where the indigenous population probably retained their superiority, and of religion, through the influence of the clergy.

Phonetic developments were certainly connected with the Frankish superstratum. The aspirated phoneme *h* had disappeared at a very early date from spoken Latin; but as it played an important part in the Germanic languages it was reintroduced, and must have been used in French up to the sixteenth century. The labiodental spirant *w* was accepted, though it often developed into guttural *g* (*guerre*, *gant*). One can even think of syntactical influences, such as the anteposition of the adjectival epithet. In the Midi, the words *Castellum novum*, in that order, have given the place-name Castelnau: it can be set against the numerous Neufchâtel or Neufchâteau north of the Loire! In the same way, a later French text would normally present *se vir zoui* (*ses verts yeux*, her green eyes). This is the usual position of the epithet in the

Germanic languages. Karl Michaelsson has, it is true, denied that this anteposition – which did not persist in French – was due to Frankish influence: it is best to leave this as an open question. But it seems difficult to deny the Germanic influence on the order of words in a sentence, in such cases as '*Or suis-je venu*' (inversion), or '*Si Lodhu-uigs sagrament que son fradre Karlo jurat conservat*' ('*Si Louis conserve le serment qu'il jure à son frère Charles*' – this is a sentence from the Strasbourg Oaths! see page 92).

Thus a new state of the language was created in the Parisian basin, which kept its place among the Romance languages but was furthest from the original Latin. And thus it happened also that France was divided into two great linguistic domains.

The problem takes on a very different aspect in the Iberian peninsula. Here, the influence of the Germanic invasions was undoubtedly slight. The Vandals left scarcely any trace, and their relation to the source of the name Andalusia remains mysterious. Portuguese and Galician contain a few words that may be connected with the Suevians (thus *briutan* > port. *britar*, fr. *briser*, cf. the eng. *to break*). Even the Visigoths, who had been strongly Romanised before they settled in the peninsula, hardly left any mark there: they are represented by about ninety words that have passed into one or other of the Iberian languages, hardly any of them relating to nature or agriculture – a sign that penetration into the peasant world had been slight.

Little affected by Germanic, the peninsula was impregnated by the Arab conquest and the settlement (along with the Arabs themselves) of a great many Arabicised Berber peasants. A very abundant Arabic vocabulary was absorbed by the Iberian languages (some of it, it is true, no longer in use) – about 4,000 words, infinitely more than from any Germanic language – their rich distribution among what may be called 'the peaceful arts' is noticeable. The name for water, *wādī*, occurs in the names of several rivers, Guadalquivir (great river) Guadiana (river Anas, its former name), Guadalete (river Lethe); and the substantive *ar-ramla*, meaning a strip of sand beside a river, is the origin of the 'ramblas', the famous Barcelona promenade. Almost the whole vocabulary of irrigation comes from Arabic, also the names of many agricultural products. Certain transitions are interesting: the sp. *algodón* has given rise to occ. *alcotón* and o. fr. *auqueton*; but the latter was later replaced by *coton*, from the it. *cotone*, which was carried on into the cat. *cotó* and port. *cotão* (without incorporating the article). The lat. *praecoquus* passed into Arabic, whence it emerged again in sp. in the form *albaricoque* (→ fr. *abricot*). Many too were the borrowings from Arabic in the spheres of craftsmanship, building, furniture, trade and even administration. On the other hand the vocabulary of abstract words is poor. This does not include the scientific vocabulary, introduced by means of translations and rapidly becoming international.

It is noticeable that substantives were constructed by the addition of the article *al*. It would seem that the Mozarabs did not recognise the article as a separate grammatical entity. Linguists have found excellent reasons for this: they have invoked the fact that the Arabs themselves frequently assimilated the article before nouns beginning with *d*, *t*, *n*, and that the Berbers, who possessed no article, treated it as part of the substantive. But was not this the case with the Mozarabs themselves? The way leading to the emergence of the article in the Romance languages was to be long, as we shall see.

Nor do linguists recognise any Arabic influence on the phonetic evolution of the Iberian languages. At most, one can observe the aptitude of the Mozarabs for assimilating Arabic words with their own rhythm: this inevitably brought with it great variations in the system of accentuation. Spanish contains numerous words ending in a vowel and with the accent on the previous syllable, following the Latin system of the paroxytone: *bueno*, *digo*. But a great many oxytones also appear, like *algodón* or *albalá*; paroxytones ending in a consonant, like *almíbar*, *azúcar*; and even proparoxytones, such as *alcándara*. In the flexibility of its system of accentuation, Spanish is probably the Romance language most comparable to English.

This influence of Arabic – that is to say of a language that was not Indo-European – has greatly emphasised the divergence of the Iberian languages from the other Romance languages. However, we must note that the northern part of what is now Catalonia, which was freed from Islam about 800, almost entirely escaped its influence. Some of the differences between Catalan and Spanish are connected with this fact.

From Latin to the Romance languages

The indirect influence of the invasions was probably even more important than the contribution described above. The creation of Barbarian kingdoms, connected in theory with an emperor of the West who disappeared in 476, brought to the fore the interaction between divergent forces that were less and less under the control of Rome. The decline of urban schools let off the brake which had been slowing up the development of the spoken language. This became more popular in character, and it is possible to see a connection between the peasant mentality and such glissades of meaning as that from the lat. *minare* (to threaten) to the fr. *mener* (lead) – because flocks were herded with loud threatening cries!

The only real power remaining in *Romania* was the clergy. The administration of towns fell more and more into the hands of the bishops, and rural life was organised in parishes. The religious community, as soon as it was established, formed the firmest link between indigenous inhabitants and invaders. It concentrated the highest aspirations of a disturbed world. One can imagine the new importance acquired by 'Christian Latin', which to some extent represented a unifying factor.

Let us try, by means of a few examples, to reconstruct the evolution of the language under these very diverse influences.

Our first example concerns what used to be called the

'rhythmic *cursus*'. It was the habit of Latin writers to end their sentences or clauses with a succession of syllables having a regular rhythm, which was indicated by the alternation of long and short syllables, variously combined. M. Hagendahl has deduced that Cicero used a number of different combinations. He records that from the middle of the third century, African writers (St Cyprian, Arnobius) showed a definite predominance of combinations (such as *péctus agnóscit*) in which the accent of intensity also marked the rhythm. Even in the most literary texts, this was the sign of a tendency common to the spoken language throughout *Romania* – the distinction between long and short syllables was disappearing.

As a second example: in 1887 a fragment was published from the manuscript of a text describing a pilgrimage to the Holy Places, copied at Monte Cassino during the eleventh century; later researches led to its being attributed to a certain Spanish nun called Egeria, who must have made the journey about 415. This text has been a constant subject of study for Latinists ever since, for they consider that it faithfully mirrors the spoken language of the fourth and fifth centuries. Egeria had devoutly described a journey which was the great event of her life, yet the text is remarkable for its very simple, familiar syntax: the chief propositions are often merely juxtaposed instead of following the complicated Latin system of subordination. The order of the words is much like that used in our modern languages. The whole work gives an impression of charming and lively spontaneity, which may be judged from the following extract (10, 8.9):

> Ac sic ergo, ut coeptum opus perficeretur, coepimus festinare, ut perueniremus ad montem Nabau. Euntibus nobis commonuit presbyter loci ipsius, id est de Libiade, quem ipsum nobiscum rogantes moueramus de mansione, quia melius ipsa loca nouerat: dicit ergo nobis ipse presbyter: si

uultis uidere aquam, quae fluit de petra, id est quam dedit
Moyses filiis Israhel sitientibus, potestis uidere; si tamen
uolueritis laborem uobis imponere, ut de uia camsemus
forsitan miliario sexto. Quod cum dixisset, nos satis auidi
optati sumus ire; et statim diuertentes a uia secuti sumus
presbyterum, qui nos ducebat. In eo ergo loco ecclesia est
pisinna subter montem non Nabau, sed alterum interiorem,
sed nec ipse longe est de Nabau; monachi autem plurimi
commanent ibi uere sancti, et quos hic ascites uocant.

Thereupon, to bring our undertaking to a successful issue,
we started hurrying so as to reach Mount Nebo. On our way,
we had been directed by a priest of the neighbourhood, that
is to say of Livias, whom we had asked to come with us from
our halting-place, because he knew the region better than we
did. This priest accordingly said to us: 'If you want to see the
water flowing from the rock, that Moses gave to the children
of Israel when they were thirsty, you can see it; on condition,
however, that you agree to give yourself the trouble of
turning aside from your road at about the sixth mile.' At
these words we were seized with an ardent desire to go there;
and we turned aside from our road at once and followed the
priest where he led us. In this place there is a little church at
the foot of the mountain, not of Nebo but of another place
not as far but close to Nebo; many monks live here, truly
saintly men who are called ascetics.

The sense of movement in the translation is the same as that
which gives life to the Latin text. The passage from one to the
other is easily made. The author expresses herself almost as we
do ourselves.

A striking feature of this text is the considerable use it makes
of demonstratives, especially *ille* and *ipse*, used after or before
the substantive to which they refer. Though infrequent in
ordinary passages, they increase in number as soon as Egeria

becomes excited by describing particularly holy places; their value is thus mainly to give emphasis. They are actually most often translated by the article. In other passages *unus* is used as an indefinite article: thus *dictus* (*est*) *unus psalmus aptus loco*, 'a psalm appropriate to the place was said'. One wonders whether Egeria has provided us with the first written example of the birth of the article from the demonstrative. Her work is in fact of capital importance for the study of the origins of the article. One cannot say that the article already occurs in it: there is not yet any word specialised for that purpose. And it is most often *ipse* that lends itself to translation by the article, although (except in Sardinia, parts of Catalonia and Gascony) it was *ille* that was to evolve into the article. We are dealing only with the beginning of this evolution.

As a third example: Gregory of Tours was born about 538 at Clermont into a senatorial family, and was bishop of Tours from 573 to 594. Always destined for the Church, he was somewhat incompletely instructed in the classics and mainly educated himself by reading the Bible and the works of Christian authors. Although he concealed the fact, he was not without literary ambition but was constantly betrayed by his own ignorance, of which he was well aware. At the head of one of his works (*Of the Glory of Confessors*) he wrote: 'How can you think that clever people will welcome your work? You do not possess the resources of art; you have no knowledge of literature . . . You often put the feminine instead of the masculine . . . And even prepositions, which famous writers tell us to respect, are wrongly used by you.' Let us try to catch him out, so as to discover through him, and as it were in spite of him, the characteristics of the spoken language.

We will turn to volume ten, chapter three of the *History of the Franks*. It is the year 590. Our author has just given us an account of the election of Pope Gregory the Great. He describes the struggles between Lombards and Franks in

Italy, whither the latter had been brought by the Emperor. He adds:

> Ibique ad eos imperatoris legati venerunt, nunciantes adesse exercitum in solatio eorum, dicentesque quia: 'Post triduum cum eisdem venimus, et hoc vobis erit signum. Cum videritis vellae huius, quae in monte sita est, domus incendia concremare et fumum incendii ad caelos usque sustolli, noveritis nos cum exercitu, quem pollicimus, adesse.' (ed. Arndt–Krusch, p. 411)

> The Emperor's envoys came to look for them there and told them that an army was coming to their help, adding: 'In three days' time we shall come back with it, this will be the signal for you: when you see the houses of this village, which is situated on the mountain side, ablaze with fire, and the smoke from that fire rising to heaven, you will know that we are arriving with the promised army.'

A very large number of errors or distortions are collected together in this passage, considered by the standards of the literary Latin that Gregory wished to write. The substitution of *vellae* for *villae* shows the increasing confusion between the two sounds. In the same way it appears that *concremare* was written for *concremari* (passive); *incendia* has been taken for the ablative feminine singular of this word, which was actually neuter and which occurs immediately afterwards in its regular genitive form, *incendii*: it could be maintained that it is the accusative plural, but it would hardly be logical to use the word in the singular and plural in the same sentence. Besides this, this passage contains several examples of the classical infinitive proposition (*adesse* twice, *concremare*, *sustolli*) which remained a predominant feature in Gregory's writing; but it also contains a *dicentes quia* which, with *dicentes quod*, represents a new form of the declarative subordinate, destined to prevail in French.

One could point to many more of Gregory's errors. Above all, there is a lack of clarity in his ideas themselves. His errors become particularly frequent when he has to choose the accusative or ablative after prepositions like *in*, *sub*, so as to indicate whether there has or has not been movement towards a certain place. 'He pays no attention to the difference between an action completed in one place and an action that implies change of place; he cannot feel the need to convey this difference.'[6] Gregory's capacity for lucid thinking deteriorated, and he afterwards became incapable of making use of the subtlety offered him by Latin as a linguistic implement! But even if such confusions disturbed the traditional rules of literary Latin, they did not create a new literary language.

After Gregory of Tours, there was hardly an author with comparable literary pretensions except in England. Most of them were notaries, writing a type of Latin more or less fixed by a use of formularies contaminated by the habits of the spoken language. After studying some fifty original documents (royal diplomas and private charters) of the Merovingian epoch (between 625 and 751), Mlle Vielliard notes an increase in 'vulgarisms'. It seems that classical Latin orthography corresponded less and less with the actual pronunciation of the words, and the scribes consequently departed from it more and more. Confusion increased among the declensions and conjugations, and the neuter gender gradually disappeared. The habit of using prepositions instead of simple inflexion became more general, while *ille* was often made to do the work of an article; in conjugation, compound tenses using auxiliary verbs became more prevalent. The infinitive proposition disappeared. Many other phenomena could be quoted here, all bearing witness to the increasing disintegration of the link with classical Latin.

We have tried to conjure up the complex development of

the spoken language between the third and eighth centuries with the help of some written texts. It was the product of phenomena common to the whole of *Romania*, under pressure of identical general conditions everywhere. Some of these phenomena seem mainly negative: the impoverishment of the range of spoken sounds, exclusive predominance of the accent of intensity, morphological confusions. Others were rearrangements of materials and habits, so that they could be consciously and systematically used in a new state of the language: such was the growing use of pronouns or demonstrative adjectives (in the future sense of the article), of nominative personal pronouns, prepositions, and simplified syntax.

Besides this, factors peculiar to each region affected phonetic development, formation of current vocabulary, and morphology. The effect of the old substrata and of the recent superstrata were combined in these changes. It was not a case of a single vulgar Latin tongue splitting up into new languages, but of increased divergence between dialects, to a point where regroupments took place.

We find ourselves once again faced with the question with which this chapter began: 'at what period did Latin stop being spoken?' The two extreme stages can be fairly clearly distinguished: in about 300, and still in about 500, the language that was spoken everywhere deserves a unique name, it was still Latin (even if some linguists prefer to call it proto-Roman); in about 800, in northern France (and later on elsewhere) the opposition between Latin and the spoken language was recognised even by contemporaries.

Secondly, methods of relative chronology make it possible to trace the phenomena of phonetic divergence for a long way back. The transition from *i* to *e*, and from *u* to *o* had certainly taken place by the middle of the first century; the former became general after 150 and did affect Sardinian, which was isolated by then; the latter became general after 250 and did not affect Romanian. In Gaul, about the year 200, the multiplication of syncopes, and the creation also of an unvoiced final *e* in proparoxytones distinguished the development of northern Gallo-Latin; for it was here alone that the palatalisation of *k* and *g* before *a* (*caru* > *chier*) was to be found at the beginning of the fifth century. A true linguistic community no longer existed in Gaul.

But it was probably not until about 600, when linguistic changes became general, the great families of Gaul no longer received classical education, and culture developed in a new key, that actual rupture took place – a rupture with the past, and a rupture between languages. But there is only limited interest in recording discontinuity in an evolutionary process which was in reality slow and continuous!

Development of the Germanic languages

When, about 800, the existence of a spoken Romance language, distinct from Latin, was recognised by contemporaries, the first written monuments to the English and German languages had just been completed. Their periods of formation practically coincided. In 813, a formula issued by the Council of Tours emphasised this parallelism: it was the order to translate sermons *in rusticam Romanam linguam aut theotiscam*, 'into the popular tongue, Romance or Germanic' (see page 91). Here, then, as in *Romania*, signs of linguistic divergence were apparent. Nor were these Germanic languages unaffected by Latin influences. Finally, and most important, the role of Christianity is recognisable in both.

The clearest example of these divergences is probably provided by what is known as the second consonantal modification in 'High German'; an important factor in the derivation of modern German. It only affected a small number of consonants, the unvoiced occlusives (*p*, *t*, *k*), and that in a variable manner according as to whether they were placed at the beginning (Anlaut) or in the middle (Inlaut) of a word. To give an extremely simplified description of this phenomenon:

t in an initial position (or after a consonant) developed into *ts* (written *z*). Thus got. *tuggô*, o. s. *tunga*, o. h. ger. *zunga* (modern *Zunge*; compare eng. *tongue*); or got. *hairto*, o. s. *herta*, o. h. ger. *herza* (modern *Herz*; compare eng. *heart*). After a vowel it developed into *zz* (which in the twelfth and thirteenth century was confused with *ss*): got. *itan*, o. s. *etan*, o. h. ger. *ezzan* (modern *essen*; compare eng. *to eat*). The phoneme *t* is the one most definitely affected by this development.

p in an initial position (or after a consonant) developed into *pf*. Thus o. s. *plegan*, o. h. ger. *pflegan* (modern *pflegen*; compare eng. *to play*). After a vowel it developed into *ff*: o. s. *opan*, o. h. ger. *offan* (modern *offen*; compare eng. *open*).

k is hardly affected in an initial position or after a consonant. Thus got. *drigkan*, o. h. ger. *trinkan* (modern *trinken*; compare eng. *to drink*). After a vowel, on the other hand, it developed into *hh* and then *ch*: got. **brikan*, o. h. ger. *brehhan* (modern *brechen*; compare eng. *to break*). Here we have the least definite and least complete evolution.

This phenomenon was definite in the south, but degenerated farther north. Simplifying somewhat crudely, one might fix its limits by what is called 'the Benrath line', running from the neighbourhood of Aix-la-Chapelle to south of Frankfurt-on-Oder (see the map on page 119). South of this line, which certainly moved northwards after the Middle Ages, lay the domain of High German dialects, which were the origin of modern German. To the north were Low German dialects, which are still spoken by millions of individuals, and have had real literary importance. The expression Middle German is used to refer to a transitional zone. The origin of this divergence, which took place between the middle of the sixth and the eighth century, of course sets a very difficult problem.

Some linguists, such as Baesecke, have insisted that the causal sequence was phonetic, and seen in this mutation a tardy result of fixing the accent on the first syllable. But why did this only happen in these High German countries, which represented the most advanced settlement of the Germans from the north-east? Or perhaps we must see it as the effect of the substratum of Celtic or Rhetic populations conquered by the Germans. Or else we must simply accept the fact that, once removed as far as possible from their original bases, and subjected to environmental influences, these southern Germans became innovators and followed distinct lines of their own. An explanation which unfortunately remains superficial in character.

But let us look at the position of the Franks. Frankish dialects had their place in High German and Middle German zones. They were found south of the linguistic limits of Germany, and also north of the line dividing Gaul. The Franks were to a large extent the creators of German, as they were of modern French. This is what might be expected from the dominant position they occupied for several centuries.

The position of Anglo-Saxon, or Old English, in relation to the High German mutation was similar to that of Old Saxon on the continent. However, after the fifth century, when Angles, Jutes and Saxons left the continent to settle in England, their closely connected but not entirely similar languages began to lead independent lives. This new insularity was marked by the formation of their own vocabulary, rather than by phonetic or morphological developments. In a well-identified collection of 3,575 words belonging to the Old English lexicon, nearly half (exactly 1,768, or 49 per cent) came from their common ancestor Germanic, but 16 per cent (558) were only found in Old English, and represented formations of their own, made after the fifth century. There were few borrowings among them: hardly any from Celtic, for the Celts had been annihilated, or driven back, or reduced to a position of great inferiority; and probably very few from Latin.

Thus we come to the problem of the early influence of Latin on the Germanic languages. Modern German provides the most illuminating example. Here, in fact, we have criteria by which we can judge the date of borrowings from Latin. Words of Latin origin that are found in all the Germanic languages must have been absorbed in them before the end of the second century AD. Inversely, it is more likely that those only found in continental languages were acclimatised after the departure of the Angles and Saxons, that is to say after the fifth century. Between these two extremes, nearly 400 words exist that are common to German, Dutch (at least in their early forms), Frisian and English, most of which were adopted by the Germans of the Rhineland, who were in contact with a superior form of Roman civilisation. These were borrowings made by artisans and peasants, and they existed 'underground' for a long while as popular terms, before being admitted to written usage in the eleventh century, when writers in German looked for words to popularise their biblical histories. These words were treated so completely as if they were of Germanic origin that their Latin derivation might escape the uninitiated. A good example is *Kaufmann* (merchant), *kaufo* in h.ger., which comes from the lat. *caupo*, tavern-keeper (cf. o. eng. *ceāp*, today *cheap*, and names of market towns, such as Chipping Norton): this is one of the earliest borrowings, for we also find the got. verb *káupjan* (buy) – surely very typical of frontier relationships, where the tavern-keeper sold a little of everything and must have seemed the incarnation of commerce to the neighbouring 'Barbarians'. Later on came numerous borrowings relating to trade, such as *Pfund* (from lat. *pondus*; cf. eng. *pound*, which suffered no consonantal mutation); or to architecture, an art which the Germans also learned from the Romans (thus *Wall*, from *vallum*; eng. *wall*); and to gardening, with names of plants and fruits unknown before these contacts (*Birne*, from *pirum*). Many tools and household objects were of Roman origin and their names were Latin: thus *Schüssel*, dish (from *scutella*), *Tisch*, table (from *discum*, tray) – the latter a reminder of the times when tables covered with dishes were set before the guests, and removed at the end of the meal. These words have undergone the second mutation, and were thus incorporated in the language before the sixth century.

It was in the fourth century that Christian infiltrations really made themselves felt in the Rhineland and southern Germany; England was converted under the influence of the Irish and of missionaries from Rome (led by Augustine of Canterbury) from the seventh century onwards; finally the rest of continental Germania was converted to Christianity after the eighth century through the combined efforts of the Irish and the Anglo-Saxons. This complicated series of events explains the diversity of linguistic aspects.

Here, even more than in Greek and Roman countries, Christianity produced a very profound and surprising mental revolution. The idea of a single God, who was also a Father, the idea of his reign (not to be confounded with any terrestrial rule), concepts such as temptation, sin and charity – these were notions that did not even exist in the minds of pagan Germans. The most natural thing was to adopt words originating from the Greek or Latin, and this was often what happened. To this type belong *Kirche*-church (from the Greek *kyriakón*, the Lord's house), *Bischof*-bishop (from *episcopus*) and so forth.

But the number of purely Germanic formations is striking enough. Thus the Germans, even when still pagans, soon acquired the feeling that the God of the Christians was an unnamable being, not to be compared with their own gods: at first they must have used the neuter participle **gudam*, meaning either 'the being men invoke', or 'the being to whom sacrifices are made'. Then this word passed into the masculine, a sign that the personal aspect – so characteristic of Christianity – had been better understood. The transition is best felt in Gothic where, although the word was masculine, it had not yet received the typical masculine suffix. It would be *Gott*, god.

But the Latins said *dominus deus*, and three words were successively used in German to translate *dominus*: *frô* (cf. o. eng. *frea*), which only persists nowadays in compound words like *Fronleichnam* (Corpus Christi); next *truhtîn* (o. eng. *dryhten*), based on *truht* (a troop of free fighting men, and tending to represent God as a war leader, freely followed by the faithful); finally *hêrro* (the most recent, since there is no corresponding English word) based on *hêr*, venerably old (compare, derived from *senex*, the Latin *senior > seigneur*). Thus they arrived at the 'Herr Gott' of the present day, by way of a succession of trial and error that is very suggestive.

Language enables us to follow the interplay of influences to which the Germans were subjected. Particularly strong was that of the Irish missionaries in southern Germany. They were responsible for the triumph of such words as *trûrin* (> *trauern*), to keep the eyes carefully lowered, exactly expressing the Christian attitude to mourning, as first found in the Irish monastery of Reichenau; it replaced *mornên* (got. *maurnan*; cf. o. eng. *murnan* > to *mourn*). Some of these terms were formed in a typically Irish manner. The Anglo-Saxons arrived later, were more conservative and had much less influence. The researches of Eggers into what he calls '*Süd-deutsche Kirchensprache*' (the ecclesiastic language of southern Germany), throw light on the combination of missionary influences and mentalities.

Conclusion

In about 800, the linguistic situations inside and outside *Romania* were in many ways comparable. On one hand, a common language, the result of a combination of diversely developed dialects within the Latin orbit; and on the other, forms of spoken language, diverging somewhat in the same manner from common Germanic origins. Of course in the Germanic sphere there had never existed those factors of

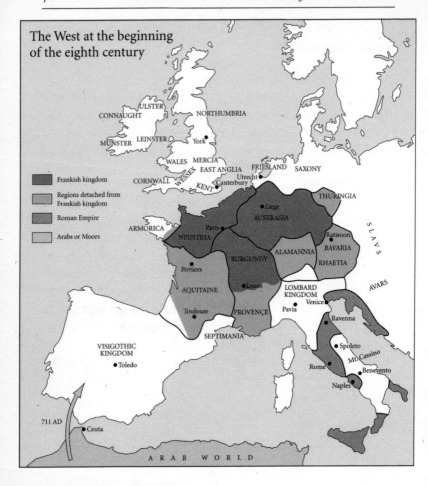

The West at the beginning
of the eighth century

Frankish kingdom

Regions detached from
Frankish kingdom

Roman Empire

Arabs or Moors

ULSTER
CONNAUGHT   NORTHUMBRIA
MUNSTER   LEINSTER   York
WALES   MERCIA
CORNWALL   EAST ANGLIA   FRIESLAND   SAXONY
WESSEX   KENT   Utrecht
Canterbury
ARMORICA   THURINGIA
Liège
AUSTRASIA
NEUSTRIA   Paris   Ratisbon
ALAMANNIA   BAVARIA
BURGUNDY   RHAETIA
Poitiers
AQUITAINE   Lyons   LOMBARD
KINGDOM   Venice
Toulouse   PROVENÇE   Pavia   Ravenna
SEPTIMANIA   Spoleto   Mt. Cassino
VISIGOTHIC   Rome   Benevento
KINGDOM   Naples
Toledo

S L A V S

AVARS

711 AD   Ceuta

A R A B   W O R L D

unification, schools, administration and literature which
brought about 'literary' or classical Latin. But when *Romania*
was invaded, these factors gradually disappeared, and the years
round 600 seem to have been particularly important in this
respect. From the very different destinies of these two branches
of Indo-European, Italic and Germanic, a state of civilisation
emerged which brought their situations closer in the course of
these troubled centuries. In about 800, with varying degrees of

precision, the more clear-headed of religions and political
leaders became aware of this position.

We must emphasise the strong element of unity represented
by Christianity and the clergy in the midst of a world where so
many factors tended towards confusion and dispersion. Inside
Romania, Christianity created a sectarian language (in no way
limited to terms relating to dogma, the liturgy or ecclesiastical
organisation), which spread and became a popular language;
it also considerably extended the role of language and contributed towards upsetting traditional linguistic hierarchies.
Outside *Romania*, Christianity spread its beliefs and ways of
thinking and feeling; it strengthened the influence of Latin on
the Germanic languages, but it also produced in the latter a
fertile creative impulse, which multiplied the links between
them and was to end in their social promotion. There is no
more clearly visible sign of this than the appearance, in the
course of the eighth century, of the first writings that can be
attributed to the English and German languages.

Chapter Four
THE TOWER OF BABEL

IN ABOUT 800, the distinction between classical, traditional Latin and the languages spoken in *Romania* had become so marked that contemporaries became aware of it. Meanwhile the Germanic languages – and not long afterwards the Slavonic languages – emerged from their 'prehistory'; their first written texts appeared. The diversity of tongues spoken on the earth's surface had always set problems for thinking men. These problems now became of practical urgency: for the first time temporal and ecclesiastical leaders had to concern themselves with them, and lay down a linguistic policy. On the whole, this consisted in preserving the primacy of Latin restored according to its classical rules, without, however, interfering with the use of 'vulgar' tongues. Thus Europe inaugurated a practical bilingualism which was to dominate her history for centuries.

Primitive ideas and Christianity

It is a primitive tendency in man to assume that only one true language exists: his own. Outside it, all is stammering confusion: an impression that the ancient Greeks and Latins conveyed in the expressive terms *Barbaroi, Barbari*. This notion does not only arise from a seemingly natural collective egocentricity. It is linked to the concept of language as magic. A name is a manifestation of the person himself: for instance, in

Australia the name of a dead child must not be used again. It is also a means of exerting power: in ancient Egypt, when the gods refused to let a dead man pass, he threatened to reveal their names to the demons. Lastly, to name things is to create them. In Gilgamesh's Mesopotamia, things appeared as fast as they were named by Apsu, the god of creation; a thing without a name had no existence. So that God created names and therefore language; he created them in such a way that there was a mysterious link between them and the objects represented by them. Language was thus creative in the second degree, it was as an intermediary between the Divine Intelligence and Reality. 'In the beginning was the Word'; so begins the Gospel according to St John, echoing the account of the Creation given in the book of Genesis.

But Christianity formulated the problem of language in a new way. By proclaiming the oneness and universality of God, and tracing the whole human race back to Adam and Eve, it set a real enigma: how had humanity passed from what must at first have been a unique language to this diversity of tongues? There are several passages in the Scriptures directly concerned with these questions. With a parallelism that Christian thinkers did not fail to emphasise, the Old and New Testaments mirror each other.

Let us begin with Genesis. The wickedness of Adam and Eve's offspring made Jehovah so angry that 'it repented the Lord that he had made man on the earth' (6, 6), and he decided to eliminate him from it. But a just man, Noah, found grace in his eyes: in obedience to Jehovah's orders, he built the Ark where he and his three sons, their wives, and a pair of every animal in existence, escaped from the devastating flood. Here we see humanity reduced again to the single nucleus of the family. The flood over, the survivors came out of the Ark and peopled the earth. Jehovah blessed Noah and his sons: 'Be fruitful, and multiply, and replenish the earth' (9, 1). In fulfilment of the Promise, Noah's sons Shem, Ham and

Japheth were the fathers of races that are set forth in detail in Genesis (10), summarising such geographical knowledge as was available in Israel at about the time of Solomon. The sons of Japheth occupied Asia Minor and the Mediterranean islands, those of Ham peopled the southern countries (Egypt, Ethiopia, Arabia and Canaan), while those of Shem occupied the regions in between. The names of seventy descendants in all appear in this passage, which commentators never got tired of studying. It is of deep significance that all the races of the Earth were described as descending from Noah.

Now follows the famous episode of the Tower of Babel (11, 1–9). It is worth quoting in full:

And the whole earth was of one language and one speech. And it came to pass, as they journeyed east, that they found a plain in the land of Shinar; and they dwelt there. And they said one to another, Go to, let us make brick, and burn them thoroughly. And they had brick for stone, and slime had they for mortar. And they said, Go to, let us build a city, and a tower whose top may reach unto heaven, and let us make a name; lest we be scattered abroad, upon the face of the whole earth. And the Lord came down to see the city and the tower, which the children of men builded. And the Lord said, Behold, they are one people, and they have all one language; and this is what they begin to do: and now nothing will be withholden from them, which they purpose to do. Go to, let us go down and there confound their language, that they may not understand one another's speech. So the Lord scattered them abroad from thence upon the face of all the earth: and they left off to build the city. Therefore was the name of it called Babel; because the Lord did there confound the language of all the earth: and from thence did the Lord scatter them abroad upon the face of all the earth.

It appears certain that this passage was not written to explain the diversity of languages. The essential idea explicitly contained in it is that the city should have been built under divine protection, for nothing could be created without God's help. Jehovah does not give way to jealousy, but he lays this down as a principle. The diversity of languages is the chosen means of punishing men, since it must prevent any more such insensate projects in the future. But the text does not state that it was bad in itself.

The eleventh chapter of Genesis ends with an account of the descendants of Shem, ancestor of the Hebrews, to whose history the Bible is from then on consecrated.

Here now are the days following the Passion – fifty days after the Resurrection of Christ. The apostles are gathered together:

And when the day of Pentecost was now come, they were all together in one place. And suddenly there came from heaven a sound as of the rushing of a mighty wind, and it filled all the house where they were sitting. And there appeared unto them tongues parting asunder, like as of fire; and it sat upon each one of them. And they were all filled with the Holy Spirit, and began to speak with other tongues, as the Spirit gave them utterance. Now there were dwelling at Jerusalem Jews, devout men, from every nation under heaven. And when this sound was heard, the multitude came together, and were confounded, because that every man heard them speaking in his own language. And they were all amazed and marvelled, saying, Behold, are not those who speak Galileans? And how hear we, every man in our language, wherein we were born? Parthians and Medes and Elamites, and the dwellers in Mesopotamia, in Judaea and Cappadocia, in Pontus and Asia, in Phrygia and Pamphylia, in Egypt and the parts of Libya about Cyrene, and sojourners from Rome, both Jews and proselytes, Cretans and Arabians, we do hear them speaking in our tongues the mighty works of God. (*Acts*, 2, 1–11)

Just as the Passion redeemed man from the burden of original sin, so the descent of the Holy Ghost effaced the effects of the confusion into which man had been thrown at Babel. It did not do this by returning to a single language, but by a mysterious inter-comprehension among God's people.

These are the fundamental texts. For centuries, it was in relation to them that thinkers approached linguistic problems. Yet their significance is not, in fact, so plain as to exclude attempts at explanations, worked out according to environment and individual temperament, and in the light of world evolution and the play of events.

Meditations of the Fathers

The experiences resulting from the crisis of the invasions were in fact very diverse. They made known, or more familiar, the languages spoken by the invaders. They made it clear that these, or their descendants, quickly accepted the Latin language once they were settled on the soil of *Romania*, thus acting as a sort of living proof of its superiority. But the fall of Rome and the collapse of traditional structures subjected Christians to agonising doubts. Had it not been asserted by the defenders of paganism that it was Christianity that enfeebled the Empire and led to its ruin? Christian writers tried to combat these accusations. They declared their faith in the providential mission of the Roman Empire, to gather all men together in their progress towards the 'City of God'. They even dared suggest that the invasions might have been a blessing in disguise, since they led to the Barbarians' knowledge of God. It was a duty too to convert those who remained outside the Empire: to communicate with them it was necessary to learn their languages, but the spread of Christianity in countries where Latin was not spoken very soon raised the practical problem of liturgical language.

The Fathers of the Church and other Christian thinkers who

lived during these troubled centuries reacted in very different ways to this experience. The question of language had cropped up in one form or another, and their reflections concerning it appeared in their writings. But their reactions were infinitely various, according to their education, temperament and environment. We will confine ourselves here to pointing out some tendencies, and referring to a few specially interesting cases.

Jerome was born in Dalmatia (*c.* 347) of a prosperous family, educated in Rome, and spent the greater part of his middle and old age in the Orient where he learned Hebrew and Greek. He settled in Bethlehem from 386 until his death (*c.* 420), and devoted himself to translating the Scriptures. He belonged to an epoch when the Romans still felt reasonably confident.

Born in north Africa (354) of a pagan father and given Christian instruction by his mother, Augustine also received a good education in his own country, and had at least a smattering of the Punic language, whose affinities with Hebrew he recognised; but his knowledge of Greek remained poor. After some years in Italy, where he was converted, he returned to Africa and was bishop of Hippo Regius (Bône) from 396 to 430. In the confusion caused by the fall of Rome he wrote his book, *De Civitate Dei* (*The City of God*). He died during the siege of his town by the Vandals. Slightly younger than Jerome, Augustine seems to have been much more severely affected by the tribulations of his time.

Isidore of Seville belongs to a period two centuries later. Born about 555, probably of an aristocratic Hispano-Roman family, he firmly took the side of the Visigothic state established in Spain at the time. In about 600 he succeeded to the bishopric of Seville, in place of his brother Leander, who had presided over the conversion of the Visigoths from Arianism. His most famous work is his *Originum sive etymologiarum libri XX,* (*Twenty Books of Origins*), a sort of encyclopedia of the ancient and Christian culture he had acquired. Its ninth book deals with languages and kingdoms. And the way he set about his task is interesting in its own right. He takes pains to discover the etymology of each word, not so much out of regard for grammar as in order to penetrate its deep significance: 'One understands the nature of a thing more easily as soon as the origin of its name is known.' His linguistic methods are in fact fantastic; but we find in his work the primitive notion that a mysterious, but real link exists between the name of a thing and its essence.

Like a great many other Fathers and writers, these men asked themselves questions about language and did their best to answer them. What primitive language was spoken before Babel? Where did all the many races come from who appeared during the general confusion of the invasions? What was the status of their languages?

The problem of the original language was not simple. Isidore hesitated to give an opinion as to the language used by God himself when he said *Fiat lux*, and created all things: yet it was with their names that existence was bestowed on them! Afterwards God spoke to the prophets, and then to the apostles, but in their own language so that they should understand him. As for Adam and the first men, the general opinion was that they spoke Hebrew. Jerome described this language as the 'matrix of all languages', without however, elaborating this judgment linguistically. Isidore accepted this view.

All races are concerned about their own origins, and tend to believe they were unusually noble, if not divine. The Germans were no exception to this rule. Christian writers pored over the tenth chapter of Genesis, attempting to connect it with all the races known to them. Hippolytus of Rome (died 235) did especially careful work on this: he placed the Romans among the builders of Babel, and completed the biblical list by including the Ligurians, the Bretons etc – ninety-five races in all. Augustine, with his knowledge of the Berber world, proved much more sceptical: races were formed and disappeared quickly; it was impossible to connect those of the fourth century AD with biblical texts. This did not prevent a number of writers calmly making out detailed and exact lists, and we owe one such to Isidore, who in consideration of the mystical significance of the figure 72, listed 72 races, as a sign of the divine harmony.

He related the European peoples to the sons of Japheth; the Gauls to Gomer, the Goths to Magog (at the cost of some bizarre etymology), the Greeks to Yavan, the Spaniards to Tubal. Then he went on to consider the names of these races: the Gauls (*Galli*) were so called because of the whiteness of their bodies (*gala* being the Greek word for milk), the Bretons (*Brittones*) because of their brutishness (*bruti* in Latin) and so on. However fantastic such lucubrations may appear, an important conclusion could be drawn from them: the languages spoken in Isidore's time were the very same that God created at the time of Babel, or were at least derived from them. What then was their status?

It is here that the most noticeable differences of opinion appear. If the confusion men were thrown into by the diversification of languages was a punishment, did it follow that these languages were in themselves bad, or at least inferior to the previous unique language? The answer was not self-evident. However, there was a general idea that what had been lost among these diverse tongues was the essential and primitive bond which had united a thing and its name ever since the time of the Creation. The languages created at Babel were arbitrary and had no connection with things. This pessimistic view could lead to several different attitudes. First, there was a longing to get back that original unity. Of course it would seem very difficult to realise it absolutely; but at least it might be possible to adhere to a few languages specially distinguished by their links with the history of the chosen people and of the redemption of man. These were the three 'principal languages' referred to by Hilaire de Poitiers (*c.* 315–67): namely Hebrew,

Greek and Latin, which had in turn played their part in spreading the Word of God. Their excellence had been established at the time of the Passion: 'And Pilate wrote a title, and put it on the cross. And the writing was, JESUS OF NAZARETH THE KING OF THE JEWS . . . and it was written in Hebrew, and Greek, and Latin.' (*St John*, 19, 19–20). Ever since then, the Barbarian peoples had received the Gospel each in their own language. But the three chief languages still retained their privileges. It can be seen as a reflection of the superiority-feelings of the Romans. We find it again in Jerome.

There was another possible attitude. This was a form of relativism, clearly expressed by Augustine: every language was changeable and imperfect, and no language was superior to the rest. This also was the evidence of the Pentecost: the apostles did not speak a single language that had miraculously become comprehensible to all – they spoke all languages. The same was true of the Church considered as a unity, and in this sense all languages belonged to every Christian. The only language that could be called Barbarian was that which still failed to praise God. Of course Augustine held Hebrew, Greek and Latin in particular esteem, as the languages of religion, wisdom and the state respectively. But none of them seemed to him truly bound to the Church. This attitude expressed a universalism quite distinct from a unitarian tendency.

This relativism was even susceptible of scientific extension. The transition is to be seen in Boëthius: he remarks that after language lost its identity with things at Babel, each developed according to the characteristics of the different races who spoke it. A fruitful idea, but several centuries were to pass before it was exploited.

These different currents of thought are found, mingled together, in Isidore of Seville. On one hand the unitarian tendency led to his using for the first time the expression the 'three sacred languages' – not sacred in themselves, of course, but because of the part they had played historically. He was aware that a language is an intimate part of a race, however, and that Latin must not be forcibly imposed on the Barbarians. He even showed some degree of relativism in that he realised that the Latin of his own time was passing through a period of decline.

Until the seventh century the controversy remained chiefly theoretical. But then the division between Latin and the Romance languages became apparent. Then it was that, partly under the influence of Christianity, several Germanic tongues were promoted to the dignity of written languages. In about 800 the problem of language became a practical one of government that had to be solved by the religious and political authorities. They approached it from the standpoint of the considerations we have described above.

The Carolingian period

Charlemagne's influence seems to have been of capital importance in this, as in so many other domains. Descended from a noble family that had replaced the Merovingian kings at the head of the Frankish State, he increased his realm by almost continual wars throughout his long reign (768–814). The greater part of the western Christian world as far as the Elbe and the Saale was thus united under his rule: the Germanic races occupied a large area, alongside the Romance peoples. Born a Frank, and devoted to the traditions of his race, he was all the same crowned Roman emperor by the pope in 800, thus becoming the first 'Barbarian' to wear the imperial purple. Out of a lively sense of his responsibilities as a Christian emperor, he gave orders for the opening of schools where the clergy could acquire the rudiments of learning, and also an exact knowledge of dogma with which to instruct his Christian subjects. Teaching was given in Latin in these schools, and even if there were few of them in all, their existence meant that workshops of copyists must be opened, text-books produced, and libraries founded. The basis for all these activities was a serious study of Latin grammar. The result was what has been called the 'Carolingian renaissance'. From a linguistic stand-point, and judging by the criteria of classical literary Latin, the description is certainly apt: the language of documents and other manuscripts became more correct, and literary works again began to be produced.

We have the evidence of Einhard that Charlemagne himself had learned enough Latin to speak it fluently. But he did not despise the Frankish tongue:

> He also had copies made, so that the memory of them should not be lost, of very ancient Barbarian poems, wherein the history and the wars of the old kings were celebrated. Besides this, he outlined the grammar of the national language. He gave to all the months names from his mother tongue, whereas hitherto they were spoken of among the Franks, some by their Latin, others by their Barbarian names; he did the same for each of the twelve winds. (chap. 29)

Einhard copied out these names of the months and winds. Except for this, unfortunately, nothing remains of the work sponsored by Charlemagne.

The question of what language should be used for religious worship and prayer must certainly have been discussed. As with the establishment of a definite text of the Bible, Charlemagne showed his unitarian leanings: he had the Roman liturgy adapted by Alcuin, who added to it certain Frankish and Spanish prayers and rituals, and he gave orders that this liturgy was to be used throughout the Empire. There remained the domains of prayer and sermons. Several canons in Council, in opposition to the over-simple desire to impose the use of Latin, show us how much discussion there must have been on the subject. The Synod of Frankfurt (794) declares: 'that no one believes that God should only be worshipped in the three languages. God is worshipped, and man's prayers heard when his demands are just, in every language.' And here is the often quoted decision of the Council of Tours (813): 'Let each man take care to translate these homilies clearly into the vulgar Roman or Germanic tongue (*in rusticam Romanam linguam aut theotiscam*), so that everyone may more easily understand what is said therein'. 'The birth certificate of national languages', exclaimed Von Wartburg: yes, in the sense (certainly intended by that writer) of an official announcement by the authorities of a birth that has been reported to them.

Such seems to be the balance-sheet of the period of Charlemagne's reign, important as it is in so many respects. On the one hand, the impulse given to education, and soon afterwards to literature, led to a return to classical traditions, and the use in writing of a Latin that roughly conformed to the grammatical standards set many centuries earlier. On the other, linguistic developments and the spread of Christianity brought the realisation that there was a place for the 'vulgar tongues', Romance and Germanic, a place which steadily grew larger from that time.

After Charlemagne, these opposing tendencies were expressed with increasing vigour. In spite of the disturbance caused by fresh invasions, particularly those of the Normans, educational and literary activity went on, and produced its most splendid fruits under Charlemagne's successors. An intense attachment to Latin developed. Educated by clerics in Aquitaine, Louis the Pious spoke Latin as his mother tongue. Did he despise the pagan poems, particularly those in the Frankish language, that he had learnt in his youth (Thégan, ch. 19)? Be that as it may, he seems to have encouraged the author of the *Heliand*, who dedicated this Christian poem written in old Saxon to him. His counsellor, Benedict of Aniane, insisted that Latin should be the sole language of clerical life: he even forbade his monks to speak their mother tongue, probably to improve their knowledge of Latin. A curious character called Smaragdos, possibly an Irishman, Abbé of Saint-Mihiel in Lorraine in about 820, went so far as to declare that Latin was a sacred language. He believed that the Latin text of the Bible had been written under the inspiration and, as it were, dictation of the Holy Ghost, and he therefore accorded it supreme authority even as to matters of grammar. What did it matter if classical Latin, as codified by the grammarian Donat, used the word *scalae* in the plural, to mean 'ladder': *scala* in the singular figured in the Latin text of the Bible. 'We will not follow Donat, because we have a more powerful authority in Holy Writ.'

At the other extreme, linguistic developments aroused the interest of a writer like Nithard, Charlemagne's grandson, who, in describing the wars between the sons of Louis the Pious, translated the text of the Strasbourg Oaths, pronounced on 14 February 842 by Charles the Bald in German and by Louis the Germanic in French, so as to be mutually understood by their soldiers. It is accepted that Nithard thus provided us with the first written monument in the French language.

The second half of the century saw important enterprises begun and decisions made. In 863, two brothers called Cyril and Methodius were sent from Constantinople to convert the Slavs of Moravia: born in Thessalonica, they had been in contact with Slavonic races, and learned enough of their spoken language to create an alphabet representing the sounds, based on Greek letters; after which they were able to translate a minimum of biblical and liturgical texts into Slavonic. Their efforts met with opposition from the German invaders, who attacked this usage of a Slavonic liturgy. The controversy was taken to Rome and put before Pope Hadrian II, one party invoking the privileges of the three languages, and Cyril replying with a list of the races 'who praised God each in their own language'. The author of the life of the missionary saint adds: 'The Pope took the Slavonic books and placed them in the church of the Blessed Virgin known as *Phatnè* and the holy liturgy was sung over them'. Without belittling the importance of the decision taken by Hadrian II (867), and confirmed later by his successor John VIII, it should be noticed that Rome was approving an initiative from the Orient, and that it was only applied to the Slavonic races.

However, it was at about the same time that Alfred the Great, King of Wessex (871–99), in spite of the tough struggle he was waging against the Normans, translated – or had translated – a series of sacred texts into old English.

Henceforth, the linguistic physiognomy of Europe was characterised by a bilingualism that involved the development of some new intellectual activities.

New intellectual activities

The humblest was probably the making of 'glossaries', as they were called. Only a minute proportion of these tools of the trade have survived, though they must once have been made in great quantities, particularly in monasteries, but a study of them does enable us to follow the development of this basic activity reasonably well. The Latin word *glossa* (from the Greek *glôssa*), which at first stood for language in general, came to be used particularly to indicate an old word that had fallen into disuse and become difficult to understand. It was later extended to notes, marginal or interlinear, explaining such words, often by giving the corresponding modern word.

The decline of knowledge of classical Latin during the seventh and eighth centuries increased the number of words that had to be explained. It became convenient to group them in glossaries, usually in alphabetical order. A good example of such a work is what is known as the Reichenau Glossary, belonging to the monastery of that name on an island in the Lake of Constance, but it was probably compiled in northern Gaul (perhaps at Corbie) during the eighth century. The first part contains 3,152 words taken from the Vulgate, in the order of their occurrence in the text. The second part is in alphabetical order and groups together words from the Vulgate and also from the Lives of the Saints and other works. Many of the modern equivalents were already 'French' in character and had moved further away from the other Romance languages: thus *arenam* is rendered by *sabulo* > *sable*, while Italian, Spanish, and the *langue d'oc* were to keep the word *arena*; also *caseum* by way of *formaticum* > *fromage* (*queso* in Spanish, *cacio* in Italian). One can see this as a precursor of our modern dictionaries – even though it was limited to words found in written texts but that had disappeared from current usage. Wherever the Carolingian renaissance was really alive, it put an end to this type of glossary. Henceforth the key to the classical Latin vocabulary was to be found in study and scholarship.

Meanwhile, really bilingual glossaries had appeared in the Germanic countries. In about 780, Arbeo, Bishop of Freising, who had been brought up in Lombardy, wanted to translate into German the somewhat unusual Latin terms with which he liked to ornament his sermons, and so had a little glossary made which was known by the first word translated in it, *Abrogans*. (At least this is the most probable attribution.) *Abrogans* means 'asking pardon, repentant'. For lack of a truly equivalent word the glossary suggested *astmot*, meaning 'humble'. How then was *humilis* to be translated? *Samftmoat* was indicated, but this really meant soft. Such groping attempts merely emphasise how far German still was from being able to render exactly the ideas and feelings beginning to take root in the consciousness of new Christians.

The Cassel glossary, actually to be found in that town today but discovered at Fulda, was a bridge between Latin or Roman terms on one side and, on the other, German vocables definitely affected by the Bavarian dialect. 'The Romans are stupid, the Bavarians are wise . . .' declares a characteristic phrase in the second part. It is a regular manual of conversation, reduced to fifty-six fairly short sentences. The first part contains 180 words arranged in methodical order: those concerning man, domestic animals, the house. It has been suggested that it was the result of the linguistic researches of a Bavarian monk in about 802, conducted in relation to the soldiers of a garrison in his country who came from northern Gaul (as is suggested by the form of the Roman words). As can be seen, it is a practical rather than a learned work.

Numerous Latin texts – books from the Bible, canons in Council, sermons – have come down to us with German glosses between the lines. Some were designed for schools, as is shown by the use of cyphers to hide the words from the pupils: thus each vowel was replaced by the consonant following it in the alphabet, *xxbbb* representing *uuâba*.

In some cases we find a continuous version between the lines. The earliest known example is a Rule of Saint Benedict translated at Reichenau before 800. As well as Reichenau, the Alsatian monastery of Murbach seems to have been a privileged place for this sort of work. It is thought that here, at about the same period, a skilful and rather free translation of Isidore of Seville's *Of Christian Faith, against the Jews* was made: the Latin and German texts are arranged opposite each other in two columns. This literature of translation also includes short texts currently in use, such as the Paternoster, professions of faith, and the formulas for baptism and confession, as well as more ambitious undertakings such as the *Book of the Evangelists*, a rhyming poem of more than 7,400 lines, by Otfrid, a monk of Wissembourg in Alsace.

More original works also exist, although often depending on linguistic acquisitions resulting from translation. Curiously enough, this German literature begins with a fragment of a pagan epic, the *Hildebrandslied*, describing the conflict between Hildebrand, companion to the Ostrogothic king, Theodoric the Great, and his own son. But it chiefly consisted in religious writings, like the *Heliand*, a sort of epic of the Saviour, a poem written in Old Saxon under Louis the Pious to instruct newly converted Saxons in the story of Christ, who was presented to them somewhat in the guise of a Saxon prince surrounded by his vassals. But some writers were inspired by current events, and this Carolingian literary activity ends with the *Ludwigslied*, a poem celebrating the victory of Louis III over the Normans at Saucourt (881). This activity was centred in the monasteries, particularly those of the south-west and Fulda: but nearly all the old German dialects are represented, from Bavarian to Saxon, by way of several forms of Frankish. The *Hildebrandslied* creates a somewhat disconcerting effect: characteristics of the most diverse dialects are to be found in it side by side, as if the Low German copyists had altered the High German text in transcribing it (or vice versa?).

After the end of the eleventh century there is a gap of apparent silence in German literature; a sign that the disturbed times either put an end to this activity or caused its results to vanish. It must also be seen as the result of what has been called the Ottonian renaissance. In a Germania ravaged by Slav and Hungarian invasions and threatened by disintegration, Otto I, Duke of Saxony, was elected king in 936, soon re-established royal authority and drove back the invaders. In 962 he received in Rome the imperial honours which had vanished with the decline of the Carolingians. The dynasty continued with Otto I's son, Otto II (973–83), and his grandson Otto III (983–1002). The Ottonians favoured the traditional language of the Empire. The literature that flourished at their court was in Latin, and nothing could be more typical of it than to find the writer Widukind celebrating the glory of the Saxons in that language. This silence was only broken by the monk Notker of Saint-Gall (*c.* 950–1022), nicknamed Thick-lips or the German to distinguish him from others of the same name. He had been for a long time director of the school of that monastery, but it was probably not for the instruction of future monks (which, except at the elementary stage, had to be given in Latin) that he translated not only religious works (the Psalms and Pope Gregory the Great's *Moral of Job*), but secular books (Virgil's *Bucolics*, a comedy by Terence, and the *Consolation of Philosophy* by Boëthius). He was chiefly concerned with the edification of laymen. Besides this, he insisted in one of his letters on the advantage of books being translated into the reader's mother tongue: only thus, he declared, could the text be completely understood. We are struck by the originality of his praise of new languages. Notker seems to have really mastered the German language, manipulating his instrument with ease, interrupting his literary translations with explanations, creating a philosophical vocabulary, and conveying shades of meaning.

Notker's subtle culture was not an isolated phenomenon. The painful and tentative efforts of the translators who had preceded him had not been in vain. Two very different attitudes had been apparent among them: one consisted in treating Latin freely, and rendering words unknown in German by periphrases, which made for easier reading but had its inconveniences. Thus the translation of Isidore of Seville sometimes transposed *Trinitas* into *dhea dhrii heida gotes* ('the three persons of God'), so risking a loss of theological exactness in the term. The word *Brot* still only had the narrow meaning of 'bread', instead of food in general; therefore some translators preferred to use *râd* (need), *zuht* (nourishment), or *bilîbi* (what is necessary to life) in the formula 'give us this day our daily bread', thus departing from habitual Christian usage. The other method, a literal translation strictly following the Latin, was possibly more fruitful. However, the results were sometimes painful; the German text of the Rule of Saint Benedict would often be incomprehensible without reference to the original Latin, between the lines of which it was inserted. The German language had been confined inside a sort of frame, which had given it the desired shape and consistency, but which could be removed in

Notker's day. Notker could write *unser tagelîcha brôt kib uns hiuto*; the word *brôt* had had time to widen its significance. Expressions that had at first been artificial were now integrated into German, and came naturally to him. Translating the first Psalm, ('Blessed is the man who . . . standeth not in the way of sinners'), Notker rendered 'sinners' by *dero sundigon* (instead of *dero sundigon manno*), because the use of the adjective as a substantive had been accepted in German on the model of Latin.

A similar demonstration based on the earliest English literature could probably be made. The starting impulse was given by a pagan epic poem, thought to have originated in Northumbria in about 700: it was *Beowulf*, the story of the young hero's struggles against the monster Grendel in Denmark; crowned king of southern Sweden, he kills a dragon but himself dies of his wounds. The pagan inspiration of these themes is varied by a certain Christian flavour. The 3,182 lines of this poem were based on alliteration, that is to say the same consonant or vowel was repeated at the beginning of at least two stressed syllables of each line, which necessitated the search for a varied vocabulary. English Christian literature, properly speaking, was dominated by the personality of Alfred the Great. This energetic sovereign made his kingdom of Wessex the base for war against the Norman invaders, and laid the foundations for English unity by assuring it a pre-dominant position in the island. He also felt it important to give cultural nourishment to an elite of laymen, as well as to the clergy, among whom the knowledge of Latin had declined. He took a hand in this enterprise himself, helped by a group of scholars. The texts chosen for translation varied greatly and were completed by several works written directly in English, such as Chronicles and Codes of Laws.

Here again, the disturbances of the period led to a silence of almost a century – a silence that was broken at about the same time as in Germany and with comparable mastery. Educated in

the monastery of Winchester, teacher of novices at Cerne
Abbas in Dorset in 987 and afterwards Abbot of Eynsham in
Oxfordshire, Aelfric (c. 955–1020) translated Genesis and
wrote Sermons and lives of the saints in old English. His free,
rich literary style shows the same advance as Notker's in
Germany. Some of these qualities are found also in the
Sermons of Wulfstan, Archbishop of York from 1002 to 1023.

There does not seem to have been a similar precocious
flowering in the literature of Romance. Of course it is difficult
to judge accurately from the fragments that have been preserved of what must have been a considerable output. In spite
of all, the disproportion between the Germanic and Romance
languages remains striking. In the France of *oïl*, hardly anything appeared after the Strasbourg Oaths except the *Cantilena*
of Saint Eulalia, composed in about 880 near Valenciennes,
and afterwards the poems of Clermont, as they are called,
('The Passion of Christ', 'Life of Saint Léger'), dating from
about the end of the tenth century. The land of *oc* had hardly
anything to offer but *Boecis*, written in about 1000, perhaps in
the province of Limousin, in which Boëthius figures as one of
Christ's martyrs and a vassal of the emperor! The harvest
elsewhere was even scantier. From Italy, before the year 1000,
there are only a few declarations by witnesses in lawsuits about
property, preserved in the archives of Monte Cassino; Italian
literature only came into existence at the end of the twelfth
century. As for Spain, we only have a few lines of Romance at
the end of some poems in Arabic and Hebrew: they give a
vague idea of the language of the Mozarabs.

We are driven to the conclusion that the breach between
the vulgar tongue and Latin was less wide here than in the
Germanic countries. Perhaps more laymen had access to works
written in Latin. Or else it was not felt necessary to put in
writing texts that had been recited or sung. Linguistic awareness seems to have been much less definite and vigorous.

Problems of bilingualism

During the ninth century, Europe thus entered the phase of bilingualism that was to dominate her linguistic life for several centuries. Latin was treated as a superior language, used by the Church, in intellectual life and in the administration. And the pre-eminence of Latin in literature, particularly in poetry, was recognised until the twelfth century. In fact, apart from their use in everyday conversation, the 'vulgar tongues' were slow to win a place for themselves in writing: they were mainly used for didactic purposes, for the edification of men who knew little or no Latin, and for legal use in England, a country whose ancient Anglo-Saxon laws have come down to us in its own language.

It is not easy to describe medieval Latin. A dead language? It was certainly not spoken by the majority of the population. All the same, it was used orally by scholars, the clergy and intellectuals, and as a professional and international language. A literary language? No, to be so described it must grow from 'the nourishing soil of current, living language' (Mohrmann), receiving sap and life from it. It has been suggested therefore that this medieval Latin should be called a 'stylised language', or, as the Germans say, '*Kunstsprache*': a living language that yet belongs to no ethnic community; the language of communication of the elite, based on a religious and cultural tradition; a written language first, and only secondly a spoken one. This Latin used by scholars was influenced to some extent by the 'vulgar tongues' which were also theirs, but its influence on them was very much stronger, as has been shown by the example of early German literature. It was in fact at the scholastic level that bilingualism really existed and produced most effect.

The majority of the population heard or saw Latin being used, especially in the liturgy. But all that truly existed for them was their own 'vulgar tongue'. From now on, the vulgar tongues developed sufficient individuality to be given special names. The clearest example is provided by German. Phonetically, the word *theodisce* is connected with the dialect of the Franks of the West, spoken between the Meuse and the Scheldt. It almost certainly originated in this region, as a result of the contact between Roman and Germanic populations: the latter treated the former as *walhisk* (> *welsch*) or strangers, and called themselves **theudisk*, meaning 'people of our race'. The word was probably adopted by the Romans themselves, as well as by Christian missionaries to refer to non-Romans, or pagans. But it was only in Charlemagne's reign that it acquired a significance that can be rendered by 'German'. In 788 an assembly of Franks, Bavarians, Lombards and Saxons condemned Tassilo, Duke of Bavaria, for a crime which was called *harisliz* in German, according to the official Annals of the Frankish monarchy: *quod theodisca lingua harisliz dicitur*. There was evident concern to avoid the expression 'the Frankish language', and use a term acceptable to all the Germans present. In fact 'German' writers, who remained well aware of the differences between dialects, were very slow to adopt this word: we meet it only six times (*in diutiscun*) in the whole of the works of Notker, who seems to be trying it out. Its general use belongs to a later period.

Evolution was less marked in England, and in the Romance countries it had not even progressed so far. In Gaul, from the Carolingian era onwards, a vulgar tongue, distinct from Latin, apparently existed: this was the *rustica Romana lingua* of the Council of Tours (813). More exact designations within this very general expression were not to make their appearance until much later. And this distinction itself was only made subsequently in countries where the popular language was closer to Latin, such as Italy: it is not found until Pope Gregory V is praised for his 'trilingualism' on his epitaph (999) (*usus francisca, vulgari et voce latina instituit populos eloquio triplici*).

Historians have sometimes wondered whether the bilingualism that began in the ninth century had harmful results, and whether the acknowledged pre-eminence of Latin in administrative and religious life did not slow up and hamper the progress of national languages. It is worth considering the question, even if briefly.

First of all, the men of the ninth and tenth centuries clearly did not conceive of any other solution. Even someone like Aelfric, who wrote in Old English, was just as eager to make Latin more easily accessible to laymen: this desire was responsible for his authorship of imaginary dialogues in English and Latin and a glossary of about 3,000 words. Even if, in Aelfric and Notker's day, English and German could be used with as much precision and subtlety as Latin, they still remained rudimentary instruments, without organised vocabularies or grammar. It was Aelfric who translated Priscian's Latin grammar into English, and conceived the strange idea of applying the rules to his own language: ought not grammar to be as universal as reason?

On the other hand, bilingualism seems to have corresponded with the social and 'national' reality of Carolingian Europe, and reflected it exactly. The Frankish State included the greater part of western and central Europe and its Romance and Germanic populations: the very necessities of existence suggested that a single language should be used for administrative purposes, and that could only be Latin. This problem did not of course arise in England or the Slavonic countries. And besides, would it not be an advantage for the small and scholarly elite, that was everywhere emerging from the vague, illiterate masses, to possess a common language, which would facilitate work as well as conversation? This advantage was to persist for centuries until its very roots were cut by social and national developments. It is useless to regret it, but just as useless to deny it.

Lastly, was this bilingualism intellectually hampering to the men who practised it? Auerbach has maintained that after the Carolingian renaissance, most writers were unable to express themselves really well in a Latin thus newly subjected to traditional rules. To the simple, natural styles of Cesarius of Arles and Gregory of Tours he opposes the scholarly application of Einhard and Lupus of Ferrières, and the laboured mannerism of Rathier of Liège and Liudprand of Cremona (tenth century). Clearly the easy and spontaneous use of Latin could only be arrived at by gradual degrees: it took two or three centuries for it to become a matter of second nature. But Gerbert was already a master of Latin. And this would be even more true of the great Latin writers of the twelfth century. Moreover, it was not so much the language that was to blame as the lack of intellectual dexterity of the authors themselves. Is it certain that they would have expressed themselves more fluently and elegantly in their 'vulgar tongues'?

Bloch has devoted several remarkable pages to the means of expression of the feudal world,[7] in which he emphasises the 'constant approximations' resulting from scholars having to keep passing from 'interior speech' to Latin. 'Among numerous causes probably combining to explain the lack of mental exactness that was so characteristic of this period, as we have seen, how can we avoid including the incessant interchange between the two levels of language?' The idea is undoubtedly attractive. Yet it is difficult to admit that linguistic situation can have done much more than complicate the task of minds that were naturally vague. This same 'constant approximation' was hardly known by the thirteenth century. And when intellectual development led scholars to create a strictly technical language, it was to Latin that they turned. Driven from other positions by the advance of the 'vulgar tongues', Latin adopted the scholastic style which was to be the mark of its decline.

Chapter Five
CRYSTALLISATION

IF IT WERE possible to draw a linguistic map of Europe in about the year 1000 it would produce an impression of extreme confusion. Apart from Latin, understood and used by a tiny minority, there only existed a number of more or less individualised dialects, from amongst which there were emerging, in a few places, the first attempts at new written languages – precursory signs of what was to follow. They had not yet been floated on the strong tide of social and cultural evolution.

Three centuries later, the extent of the change was clearly visible. By no means lacking in significant variety, the same phenomena were developing everywhere. Groups of dialects were converging, to the advantage of a few languages. Their use in writing was becoming commoner, both in the administrative and legal domains and in literature. Their own physiognomy was changing; linguists express this internal evolution in terms of the passage from Old French to Middle French, and from Old English to Middle English (although the dates differ from one country to another).

It is impossible to understand these linked phenomena in human terms without trying to picture that 'flowering of the West' which has so often been described. Men had become more numerous. Clearing the woods, marshes and moors that isolated human establishments from each other, tracing or improving tracks and roads to connect them, they developed a life of relationships, whose economic aspects are well known; markets and fairs multiplied and were occasions for conversation and (in the case of the great international fairs, such as those of Champagne) for dialects belonging to different linguistic families to rub up against each other. Religious life gave rise to similar encounters, thanks to pilgrimages, some of which were European in character (Saint Gilles, Compostela, Rome, the Holy Places), and to the Crusades. Whether the latter took place in Spain, on the way to the Holy Places, or even inside Christendom, they brought men who spoke different tongues into contact, and so raised problems of communication. Urbanisation was manifesting itself also, in the revival of old Roman cities and the birth of a great many new centres. The towns provided incomparably more opportunities for conversation than the country. And languages were also enriched by the appearance of new activities. It was not merely that men had become more numerous, they also talked much more and in different ways.

Society had become diversified; its articulation was more complex. An upper and middle class was everywhere developing, and playing an increasing part in human organisation. At least some of the town burgesses were occupied in administration, thus gaining a certain degree of autonomy for themselves. All these men – not only the elite of scholars and aristocratic laymen – felt the dawn of cultural needs, and wanted to satisfy them without learning Latin, for which they had little time or desire, and often no ability.

Society was in a sense becoming laicised: in the same sense that the word *laicus* was gradually losing its meaning of 'ignorant', and now referred more precisely to men who knew no Latin. There were now more kings and princes who knew no Latin or extremely little, but yet possessed real culture, and were in favour of works being written in the vulgar tongue. And many of the landed gentry followed suit. Professional requirements created an important class of judges, lawyers, notaries and scribes, who carried out an increasing number of functions formerly reserved for the clergy, and who felt the need to make contact with their clients by writing in the popular languages. Urban schools were opened all over the place, and often opposed the clergy's pretensions to control the 'insolence of the laity': the occasion at Ghent in 1191, for instance, when the Countess of Flanders allowed that 'if anyone suitable and capable wants to open a school in the town no one can prevent him', was not isolated. Of course, these urban schools did not eliminate Latin from their syllabuses. But most of the practical teaching was given in the 'vulgar tongue' needed by the sons of merchants and artisans. Even the humblest artisans and peasants usually reached a higher standard in the manual skills of their trade, and acquired the habit of applying reason to their actions: this was the culture of *homo faber*. The cultural superiority of the clergy became less obvious. In extreme cases, the pre-eminence of Latin, the position of the clergy and the authority of dogma were disputed by heretics.

Political regroupment of the future nations of Europe went on in an irregular and variable manner. It was affected by geographical factors, the weight of tradition and the result of political and military conflicts. The emergence of centralised states always constituted a valuable basis for linguistic unification. Where this was lacking, other elements had to be introduced.

The first states to be formed were the kingdoms of Sicily and England, both of them relatively small countries that had been conquered by the Normans. The latter proved to have a vocation for government, and its exercise was facilitated by conquest. England was thus soon provided with a powerful centralised monarchy, thanks to its conquest in 1066 by William the Bastard, Duke of Normandy, who took over the traditions of Anglo-Saxon royalty, and organised a feudal system with leaders recruited from among his companions.

The French contribution was afterwards several times added to, in particular when an Angevin dynasty, the Plantagenets, succeeded to the English throne in 1154.

The development of the French state followed very different lines. The work of political consolidation and administrative organisation was carried on first among the large fiefs, and after the time of Louis vi the Fat (1098–1137), within the king's domain. Thus consolidated, the Capet dynasty was able to unite all these fiefs to the Crown: Normandy, Anjou and Artois under Philippe Auguste (1180–1223), and part of Languedoc as a result of the crusade against the 'Albigensian' heretics (1229). Under Saint Louis ix (1226–70) administration and the royal prestige developed.

In the Iberian peninsula, the dominant phenomenon was the 'reconquest' of the Moorish states. As a result of this, the first place was given to those kingdoms which were carrying it into the south: Castile, originally merely a fortified border region of León, but whose sovereigns gradually occupied the whole central area of the peninsula; and then Aragon, which was united to Catalonia in 1137, and conquered Valencia in 1238. The separate kingdom of Portugal stretched to the west and as far as the Algarve. By the middle of the thirteenth century, Moorish Spain was reduced to the kingdom of Granada, which survived for more than two hundred years.

The Empire, whose titular head could still in the middle of the twelfth century look down upon the 'petty kings' of the West, had a different fate. Its widespread power, and its attempts (after the time of Frederick i of Hohenstaufen, known as Barbarossa, 1152–90) to develop its Italian and Sicilian domains so as to obtain the necessary material resources, involved the Empire in a mortal struggle with the Papacy, which encouraged the seigneurs and the towns in their resistance. The last of the Hohenstaufens, Frederick ii (1215–50), was a Sicilian, who increased concessions in Germany in order to obtain the necessary forces for his Italian policy. After his death, Germany remained until the nineteenth century a confused collection of principalities, placed under an illusory imperial power. Shared among the kingdom of Sicily, the Papal States and the territories increasingly dominated by a few large towns in the north such as Florence, Genoa, Milan and Venice, Italy too was affected by this conflict, and had to wait until the nineteenth century to be unified.

The period we are considering was not only remarkable for the 'crystallisation' of new languages. It also represented an important phase in the history of medieval Latin. It was now that the fruits of the 'renaissance' of the Carolingian epoch came to maturity. Medieval Latin was probably never written (or even spoken) more fluently and elegantly than in the twelfth century. However, from the thirteenth century onwards it appears to have been on the defensive: it was guarding what the new languages had not yet conquered, and its very nature reflected these developments.

The two French languages

Why do we begin this survey with France? Both because writing developed early in the French language, and because of the immense influence it exerted in Europe during the twelfth and thirteenth centuries. Nevertheless the case of France presents a complication: this nation which was advancing so vigorously towards political unity produced two quite distinct languages.

The origins of this linguistic duality have already been briefly referred to (page 60). Between the two languages – known as *oc* (from the Latin *hoc*) and *oïl* (from *hoc ille*), words used in the affirmative, considerable differences can be recognised: out of nineteen distinguishing criteria chosen by the linguist Ronjat, sixteen divide the two French languages, while only four separate the *langue d'oc* from Catalan, seven from Spanish, and eight from Italian. But they partly depend on the evolution of the French *langue d'oïl* since the thirteenth century.

However, some existed already, particularly in phonetics. One may note the striking evolution of *capra > cabra* (oc) and *chievre* (oïl). In the first case the accented *a* and the final unstressed *a* are both preserved, the initial consonant has not changed, and the unvoiced labial *p*, in an internal position, is sounded as *b*. In the second, the tonic *a* is diphthongised as *ie*, while the unstressed *a* is reduced to unvoiced *e*; the initial *c* is palatalised as *ch*, and the internal *p* is sounded and evolves into the labiodental *v*. This is merely an example: others could be taken from morphology. Nearly all reveal the much greater conservatism of Occitan.

Words belonging to the *langue d'oc* first found their way into legal deeds, now preserved in archives. The ignorance of the scribes was responsible: though it was their principle to write in Latin, they relapsed into isolated words or even whole passages of the 'vulgar tongue', every time their memory or their zeal failed them. Documents written about 1034 in the region of Foix, and Narbonne about 1053 have come down to us in this state. The transition to the writing of the entire deed in *langue d'oc* probably shows a new attitude of mind: we come across it in about 1100. In spite of what has been lost, more than five hundred original documents of this sort have been preserved. Their distribution cannot be explained by chance alone: it was on the southern slopes of the Massif Central, between Toulouse, Moissac, Castres, Rodez and Millau that written use of the vulgar tongue first spread.

The years around 1100 also saw the sudden appearance of lyrical poetry in Occitan, first made known in written form by the Duke troubadour William of Aquitaine (1071–1127). Thenceforward, for more than two centuries, this movement expanded widely: the works of about 460 troubadours have been preserved. We will only refer here to the diversity of their geographical and social origins – from Gascony to Limousin and Provence, from noblemen to humbler landowners and mere commoners. Yet all communed together in a strictly codified lyricism, whose rules even extended to vocabulary and syntax.

To explain this precocious and brilliant literary renaissance, it is not enough to say that there seems to have been no very vigorous revival of learning during the Carolingian epoch – a negative factor, apparent in the failings of eleventh-century scribes. An original form of culture had developed outside the world of scholarship, having its own sensibility and literary ideals. It depended on a social movement which collected together gentry and bourgeoisie in the courts of the nobility. Attachment to the Occitan language, perfected as a means of expression, was very strong in the case of heretics: when, in 1178, a mission came to Toulouse to combat it, two 'perfect' or pure Cathari presented it with a statement in Occitan; invited to speak Latin so as to be better understood, the two men professed to know none, and the discussion had to be continued in *langue d'oc*!

The map on page 111 shows the chief dialects that made up the living reality of that language. The most vigorous originality was shown by the northern dialects, Limousin, Auvergnat, Alpine (in particular the palatisation of *ca* and *ga* into *tcha* and *dja*, even in the middle of a word), but above all Gascon (which, like Castilian, used *h* instead of the initial *f*: *farina > haría*). There was also the whole domain of Franco-Provençal. But it must be stressed also that middle Occitan, covering Languedoc and Provence proper, was the most conservative and free from special developments. It could have been the foundation for a unified *langue d'oc*. In fact, we owe the only real attempt at unification during the twelfth and thirteenth centuries to the troubadours: whether Provençals, Limousins, Gascons or even Catalans and Italians, they wrote in a common language from which dialectal peculiarities had been eliminated. It is often difficult from the poetry alone to decide the geographical

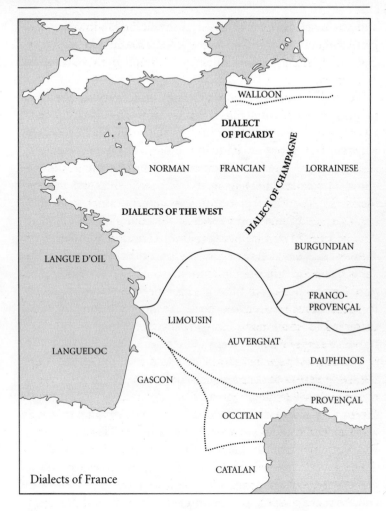

WALLOON

**DIALECT
OF PICARDY**

NORMAN   FRANCIAN   *DIALECT OF CHAMPAGNE*   LORRAINESE

DIALECTS OF THE WEST

LANGUE D'OIL

BURGUNDIAN

FRANCO-
PROVENÇAL

LIMOUSIN

AUVERGNAT

LANGUEDOC

DAUPHINOIS

GASCON

PROVENÇAL

OCCITAN

CATALAN

Dialects of France

origin of the author. A good example of literary *koinè*: but this language is necessarily somewhat artificial and could hardly survive the disappearance of its social support. Politically, the countries of the *langue d'oc* remained disunited: unity was imposed on them from without; it was the achievement of the houses of Capet and Valois. And, if the idea of a linguistic assimilation of their southern subjects was foreign to the latter, the seeds of the final triumph of the *langue d'oil* – in terms of multi-secular evolution – were present in the domination of a northern dynasty, made effective by the Albigensian Crusade.

In the country of the *langue d'oil*, the written use of the vulgar tongue had at first only been literary (apart from the Strasbourg Oaths). Epic poetry had flourished since the second quarter of the twelfth century, to be followed by court poetry, aristocratic in character; after the thirteenth century a truly bourgeois literature existed both in verse and prose. Arras was the most brilliant centre for prose; it was here too that the earliest municipal document in French appeared (1230). Liège followed in 1233, Tournai in 1235, Ile-de-France and Champagne several decades later. In 1160–70, however, the Templar's Rule was translated into French, for the use of those knights entering the order who had not had an education based on Latin. This was a linguistic reflection of the exceptional economic expansion in the Low Countries and their surroundings.

These early writings were transcribed in dialectal form. The philosopher Roger Bacon left us a picture of the dialects of the *langue d'oil* in about 1260, which could be represented today on a map with little change. In relation to what was to become the French language, these dialects show some original characteristics: thus in the dialects of Normandy and Picardy, *c* has the hard sound *k* before *a* (*car*, not *char*), changes to *tch* before *e* or *i* (and not to *ts*: *ochire*, not *ocire*, to kill), *g* is preserved (*gambe*, and not *jambe*), etc; the termination *-ie* instead of *-iée* is a Picardism that has occasionally passed into French (for instance *les Folies-Bergères* for *les Feuillées-Bergères*). Part of the historical literature of the twelfth and thirteenth centuries was Norman, part of the court poetry was from Champagne, and some bourgeois productions were Picard or Walloon. However, at the end of the twelfth century, Chrétien de Troyes, the poet of Champagne, took some pains to avoid the more specific forms of his dialect. Already the influence of Francian was beginning to be felt.

This is the name given to the dialect of the Ile-de-France. Linguists such as Von Wartburg have emphasised its 'average' character, and the absence of phonetic eccentricity which destined it to become the French language. Such considerations may always seem rather like *a posteriori* justifications. And the very different example of Castilian makes us cautious. Whatever the truth about its 'innate' suitability, the success of Francian was above all connected with that of the Capetian monarchy. But it came late: it had first to be established in the Ile-de-France and then to lay claim to authority over the whole country, and this last result was not achieved until the thirteenth century. However, in 1173, the poet Guernes from Pont-Sainte-Maxence proudly declared:

> *Mis langages es buens, car en France fui nez.*

(My language is good, for I was born in France.)

And in about 1180, the poet Conon de Béthune complained of being jeered at at Court for his Picardisms. He did so, however, in excellent Francian:

> *Ne cil ne sont bien appris ne cortois*
> *Qui m'ont repris se j'ai dit moz d'Artois*
> *Car je ne fui pas noriz à Pontoise.*

(Nor are those well educated or courteous,
Who reprove me for using words from Artois,
For I was not nurtured at Pontoise.)

But it was in the thirteenth century that royal administrative power reached almost every part of the kingdom, and the dialects of the *langue d'oïl* were eclipsed by Francian as a literary language. The growing importance of the university of Paris also contributed to its success.

Old French differs from modern French. Old French texts have a striking abundance of diphthongs, either due to the lengthening of an accented vowel (*cŏr* > *cuer* >, today *coeur*), or to the combination of a primary with a secondary vowel (*facĕre* > **fagere* > **fag're* > *faire*), or to the vocalisation of *l* (*alter* > *autre*). During the twelfth century these diphthongs began to be reduced; modern French possesses hardly any, and a better idea of an analogous auditory impression is got from Modern English (which has preserved *joy*, for example).

In morphology, the existence of a declension with two cases must be emphasised: besides the *langue d'oïl* and Occitan, only Romanian possessed it (and still does). Inflexion essentially depended on preserving the final *s* in the subjective singular and objective plural. The system of conjugations was profoundly transformed: inflexion was simplified by use of analogy, but on the other hand periphrastic forms using the auxiliary verb were developed: these triumphed completely in the passive voice, and increasingly in the active voice also.

These developments in morphology are obviously connected with those in syntax. The reduction to two cases for the substantive, did not lead so much to a multiplication of prepositions as to confusion in the notion of relationships: the objective case expressed the object, time, place and possession, all at the same time. But the reduced declension also authorised a certain freedom in the construction of a sentence: the complement was often put before the verb, and the subject after it. Simplification of verbal forms encouraged the use of the subjective personal pronoun as a means of distinguishing them: but this habit had not yet become general.

The vocabulary of Old French was mainly enriched by derivation; borrowings from foreign language were few: thus, in spite of the Norman occupation, very few Scandinavian words penetrated the French language (*bateau, étais, hune*, *vague*, *crique*). The relative rarity of 'erudite' words is easily explained. Latin remained the language of erudition, and translations were still so few that there was little need to find equivalents in French.

Moreover it was for its sweetness, rather than for its clarity and precision, that French was praised. '*Dieux le fist si doulce et amiable principalement a l'oneur et loenge de luy mesmes*' (God made it so sweet and pleasant chiefly for his own honour and praise), wrote an English author. Occitan and the *langue d'oil* both exerted a truly international influence. The Occitan language was used by many southern writers: the King of Aragon, Alfonso the Chaste (1162–96), Sordello of Mantua, the poets of the court of Frederick II of Sicily, later on Dante and Petrarch. The *langue d'oil*, backed by the spread of French chivalry and the fame of its customs, but also by the success of the trade fairs in Champagne and the reputation of the university of Paris, was also widely spoken. In England, it was the language of the Norman conquerors. In Germany, heroic poems and Court romances were translated and imitated; Wolfram von Eschenbach made fun of his own poor knowledge of French. In northern Italy, Marco Polo, returning from the circumnavigation of Asia, dictated his memoirs in French stuffed with Italianisms. The literature of these countries had to break free from the ascendancy of the two French languages, just as from the traditional authority of Latin.

England: a trilingual country

Linguistic developments in England between the tenth and the thirteenth centuries differed profoundly from those in France. 'Old English' had made a precocious written appearance during the ninth century. Two successive events, both caused by the Normans, altered a course which had appeared completely fixed.

First, a great many legal or literary texts dating from the eighth and ninth centuries familiarise us with this Old English, a language so purely Germanic that it has several aspects in common with modern German.

Phonetically, the vocalic system was based on pure vowels, without any tendency towards diphthongisation. The modern Englishman asks: *how?* His ancestors of the ninth century used to pronounce it *hū* (as in *food*). The sound *ü* has so completely disappeared from modern English that an Englishman finds it hard to pronounce, but it has persisted in German; it had its place in Old English, for instance in *fyr* (today *fire*). Among the consonants, *h* was much closer to the modern German *ach* than to the present-day English *h*. The dental spirant that we find today at the beginning of words like *thin* and *this* was already in existence: the alphabet expressed it by the signs þ and ð.

Old English possessed a rich inflective system. The declension of substantives contained no less than four cases (nominative, genitive, dative, and accusative), which could be supplemented when necessary by an instrumental case. And several types of declension existed. Adjectives were subject to weak or strong declension, according as they were preceded by another word or not (as in modern German). There was a demonstrative, foreshadowing the article: it could take twelve different forms, according to gender, number and case! The table of conjugations is somewhat disconcerting: there were only two tenses, present and past, the future tense of Germanic being replaced by the present; and there was a complete system of personal inflexions, none of which remain today except the -*s* of the third person singular in the present tense.

This abundance of inflexions necessitated a certain flexibility of syntax. The order of the words resembled that of modern German: inversion whenever the sentence began

Dialects of Old English

with an object, an adverb etc; relegation of the verb to the end in subordinate clauses.

The vocabulary of Old English was purely Germanic; it owed almost nothing to Celtic, and although its borrowings from Latin were noteworthy (about 450 words) there was strong resistance to it: even in the religious domain, if a suitable alternative existed it held its own against the Latin term. The ease with which derivatives and compounds could be formed also meant that the vocabulary could be readily enriched. In any case, many Old English words disappeared

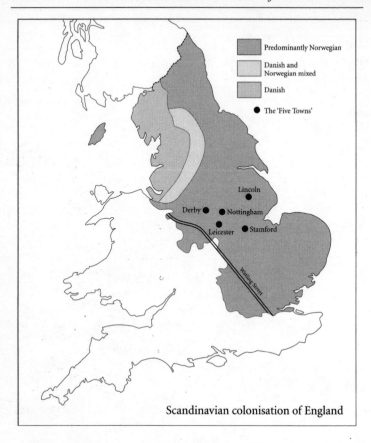

Scandinavian colonisation of England

after 1066: out of a random selection of 2,000 it has been calculated that about 535 survive in modern English.

Secondly, the flowering of Old English had at first been favoured by the repeated Danish raids on the North Sea coast, beginning in 793. Leader of the resistance to the Danes, Alfred the Great had also brought about the triumph of his own west Saxon dialect in the domain of writing. He was, however, obliged to yield ground to the invaders in the end – the Danelaw, or roughly the whole north-eastern section of the island. Their settlements are revealed by place-names of

Languages of Germany

Low German

Middle ⎱ High German
Upper ⎰

Frisian

Sorabian (Slav)

German linguistic frontier

Boundaries between low, middle and upper German

Königsberg

EAST LOW GERMAN

Hamburg

Berlin

LOW SAXON

Wittenberg

LOW FRANKISH

Benrath

Leipzig

Brussels

Cologne

FRANKISH

Meissen

HIGH SAXON

SILESIAN

Mayence

Prague

Trier

Heidelberg

Nuremberg

ALAMANNIC

Augsburg

Vienna

St Gall

BAVARIAN

Chur

Scandinavian origin, indicated by suffixes like *-by*, village, farm (Derby, Rugby), *-thorpe*, hamlet (Bonthorpe), *toft*, estate, farm (Lowestoft) – including more than 1,400 place-names in all. But the linguistic influence of the Danes was not confined to these.

Fear of the pagan Danes remained very much alive among the Anglo-Saxons and delayed fusion. But the spoken languages were close; numerous words such as *wife*, *summer* and *to sit*, were common to both. There were a great many popular borrowings, but they remained oral for a long time and did not appear in texts until many centuries later. Their expressive content is more striking than their number (about 900). They include such words as *law*, *to call*, of which the first instances date from the tenth century. In the eleventh, the verb *to take* replaced *niman* (cf. the German *nehmen*), and *to die*, *knife* and other words appeared. *Bond*, *fellow*, *guest*, *husband*, *leg*, *skill*, and the adjectives *awkward*, *big*, *ill*, came later. We notice form-words, like the preposition *till*, the conjunction *though* and the pronouns *same*, *they*, etc. Some English words changed their form under Scandinavian influence (*bird* > *birth*, *swester* > *sister*), or sometimes their sense: thus *dream* first meant *joy*; and *plough* stood for a measure of land. All this shows the popular, and as it were intimate character of Danish penetration.

Several thousand Scandinavian words were absorbed into northern dialects but got no further. There were even phonetic influences, such as the preservation of the hard *g* in an initial position: while Chaucer, who was a southerner, was still writing *yive* in the fourteenth century, it was the northern pronunciation and orthography *give* that prevailed.

Some linguists even attribute to the Danes the changes in the inflective system, preserved with such profusion in Old English. The Danes also possessed their inflexions, but they were not the same as those of the English: in the interests of mutual comprehension, each may have abandoned some. However accurate this explanation may be, it is certain that, in the gradual elimination of the inflective system, the northern dialects were ahead of those of the south by at least half a century.

Anglo-Saxon and Danish contingents fought side by side at Hastings in 1066. Hardly had this fusion begun to be realised than the Norman conquest supervened: but this time the conquerors were Gallicised Normans.

Thirdly, the conquest of 1066 was as important linguistically as politically, but its results were more complex than they might appear at first sight. The conquerors did not all speak the same language (there were Flemish soldiers fighting beside the Normans), and their numbers were small. It is true that, faced by stubborn native resistance, William conferred important posts in the administration and clergy on his followers, and transferred a great many properties to them. So that the new arrivals filled almost all the 'upper ranks' in the country. But the conquerors, with the king at their head, tried to insinuate themselves into English traditions; William Rufus (1087–1100) got help from the English several times against his undisciplined feudal dependants. In about 1180, the *Dialogue of the Exchequer* declared: 'nations are so mixed, that it is difficult today to discern which freemen are of English origin and which Norman'.

And the course of history continued to bring Frenchmen to England. In 1154, Henry II Plantagenet, Count of Maine and Anjou, and Duke of Aquitaine by his marriage, ascended the English throne. England was now merely one element in vast dominions that were mainly French. French marriages, and the resulting immigration of the nobility from Poitiers or Provence, the part played by Gascon merchants in English trade – all this reinforced the French contribution, and inspired a form of xenophobia even among the highest ranks of the aristocracy. By about 1180 the country was sufficiently Anglicised for assimilation to go on naturally.

Although many works have certainly been lost, literary evolution followed the same lines. It is true that during the decades following the Norman conquest little literature in English was produced – but not much more in French. Latin was generally adopted as a literary language. From the end of the twelfth century, a fairly important literature in French began to be produced, but the same can be said of English too: *Brut*, an epic poem by Layamon, and works like *The Owl and the Nightingale* were written for an aristocratic public, capable of understanding and appreciating them. Indeed there was so much that was new about the language they were written in, that linguists generally treat 'Middle English' as having started about the middle of the twelfth century. It was a sign that English had never stopped being freely spoken.

This leads us to the problem of the oral use of language in daily life. We try to solve it from the anecdotes contained in literary and historical works, coupled with a certain amount of generalisation and hypothesis. English was certainly still the language of the people, though bilingualism also sometimes occurred. The history of the writer Orderic Vital is remarkable. Born in England in about 1075, he was the son of a Norman priest and an Englishwoman, and was sent to school in Normandy at ten years old: there he first came into contact with the French language, proving that his parents had spoken English to each other. On the other hand a chronicler records that one of the tenants of Samson, Abbot of St Edmunds, understood no French, indicating that the others must at least know a few words. One of the charges preferred against William of Longchamp was that he had sent for minstrels from France to sing his praises in the streets – a form of personal advertisement which would only have been effective if it was generally understood.

Bilingualism also spread very quickly among the secular elite: Henry 1 (1100–35) and, much later, Edward 1 (1272–1307), were the only kings who spoke English, though others must have understood it. But the nobility, uncultured though they were, soon became Anglicised. Simon de Montfort, Earl of Leicester, knew no English at all when he arrived in the country; yet after the victory at Lewes (1264) the party of barons led by him talked of putting to death anyone who could not speak English.

Finally, a good many examples of trilingualism were to be found among the clergy: Layamon, author of *Brut*, a simple parish priest, tells us that his poem had Latin, French and English sources; Stephen Langton, Archbishop of Canterbury from 1207 to 1216, wrote his *History of Richard I* (now lost) in

Latin; he was also responsible for the earliest private letter written in England in French, and he preached in English. It would be easy to multiply examples.

We must therefore be careful not to exaggerate the effects of the Norman conquest. Even before 1066, there were many Frenchmen at the court of Edward the Confessor. After 1066, the newcomers quickly became Anglicised. English finally emerged victorious from a long co-existence, whose partial coincidence with social categories is striking.

Naturally both the French and English languages were marked by this prolonged co-existence. For a hundred years or so, the French spoken in England was close to the Norman dialect. Then the diversity of origin of immigrants, and the increasing influence of English gave it an eccentric physiognomy. In the thirteenth century, Walter Map made fun of 'Marlborough French'; while Gervase of Tilbury shows us the nobles sending their children to Normandy to learn good French.

The English language was also affected by French, particularly as to vocabulary: a great many French words were borrowed. These borrowings always appear rather later in texts. However, by the thirteenth and fourteenth centuries they had increased: having survived the crisis of 1066, English opened its doors to French influence. It is agreed that the English language today includes twice as many words derived from Latin and French as from Germanic, though the latter are in more ordinary use. This is not an absolute rule, since the extremely common adverb *very* originates from the French adjective *verrai* (*vrai*, true). But the borrowed words belong to well-defined domains: government (where the invaders hardly respected more than the words *king*, *queen* and *earl*), administration, law, the army, the Church; they also apply to fashionable life, clothes (*fashion*, *dress*, *button*), jewels (*jewel*, *pearl*), food (*beef*, *mutton*, *bacon*, *sugar*, *roast*), pleasures (*leisure*, *chess*), hunting; and finally to the arts, philosophy and sciences. It was the language of the upper class, and penetrated English along with them. What took place was a true assimilation, displacing the accent on some words (*mariáge > márriage*). Pairs of words of Germanic and French origin persisted and maintained subtle semantic differences: for instance, *ask* and *demand*, *wish* and *desire*. And we know that the Germanic sheep alive in its field, became French (*mutton*) on a dish. In spite of all, a large part of the ancient English vocabulary was swept away by this invasion.

It does not follow that the influence of French was purely lexical. It is unlikely that the language of a minority had much effect on English phonetics. But as for syntax, apart from French turns of phrase like 'to take leave', sometimes marked by the postposition of the adjective ('the body politic', 'from time immemorial'), it is possible that French influence often placed the verb in the middle of the sentence. In prosody, imitation is obvious. But at all events, French influence was not solely responsible for the 'middle English' spoken and written from the twelfth century, and differing in so many respects from Old English.

Difficulties in the path of German unification

Much larger than England, and lacking a historical tradition such as that of Gaul, Germania was bound to be the scene of a long and difficult linguistic synthesis. Charlemagne's efforts at unification, and the missionary activity of the Church had encouraged writing in the vulgar tongue, which manifested more or less marked dialectal characteristics. The authors were aware that they were writing in Frankish, Bavarian or Saxon, rather than that their dialects genuinely had much in common. Notker used the word *deutsch* with caution. Eggers declares that old German was not yet a formed language at this stage, it was merely *werdendes Deutsch* (becoming German). The task of gradually creating the language was achieved by the different dialects assimilating in common the classical and Christian inheritance under the influence of Latin and its rules.

However, during the eleventh century, the concept of a 'German' language seems to have imposed itself, at least on cultured circles. The word *deutsch* reappeared in the *Annolied*, an epic poem written about 1090, probably in the monastery of Siegburg, to celebrate the noble deeds of Anno, Archbishop of Cologne. It deals not only with *diutischin sprechin*, but also with *diutischemi lande*, the German land to which the common language belonged. The *Annolied* can be considered as the birth-certificate of German, since this concept never again disappeared. The *Kaiserchronik*, written at Ratisbon and ending in 1150, uses this word *diutisk* freely in its various senses. It was taken up by the Court poets, who, according to Walter von der Vogelweide, defined the German land thus:

> *von der Elbe unz an den Rîn*
> *und her wider unz an Ungerland*

> (from the Elbe to the Rhine,
> and thence to Hungary).

This self-discovery was connected with the glamour attached to the idea of empire at the time of the Salian emperors, and afterwards with those of the house of Hohenstaufen up to about 1250; they stood for a tendency to political unity. Since they considered themselves heirs of the Roman Empire, their activity was expressed mainly in Latin, whether in the daily work of the Chancellery or in great histories of the period: it was in Latin that Otto of Freising, uncle of Frederick Barbarossa, celebrated the noble deeds of that hero. Nevertheless, after the eleventh century, an increasing number of works of all sorts were written in the German language. Religious literature, still founded on translations, was enriched with sermons and sacred poems. Epic and lyric poetry was written for the nobility of the 'ministerials' (the state officials), and their authors were knights. Not all this literature has been preserved: some has been lost, and many of the secular works were not judged worthy of transcription. We have therefore only an indirect acquaintance with epic poetry, lively though it certainly was, until the poem of the *Nibelungen* was written at the end of the twelfth century. Only then did this reticence disappear: a sign of change in tastes and ideas, but also of a fresh attitude to the vulgar tongue.

Because of the part played by the clergy and the emperor's lack of a fixed residence, this literary activity took place in a great many different centres, and was expressed in different dialects. Their linguistic relationship was, however, clearly apparent, and writers tried to eliminate the more troublesome dialectal peculiarities in order to be better understood. Such was the general character of the period qualified as 'Middle' by German linguists, which lasted from the beginning of the twelfth century until the end of the fifteenth.

It may be convenient to give an example, illustrating some characteristics of Middle German, at least in its first stage. Let us take the beginning of the *Credo*, as it is found translated in the Wissembourg Catechism (about 800):

Gilaubiu in got fater almahtigon, scepphion himiles enti erda (I believe in God the Father almighty, maker of Heaven and Earth).

In the Millstatt Psalter, composed about 1180, this passage has become: *Iche geloube an got vater almaehtigen, schephaer himels unde der erde*.

The comparison is instructive: it enables us to indicate some of the progress that had been made:

1 The consonants had changed very little except for the passage of *sc- > sch-* (*scepphion > schephaer*).

Simplifying considerably, it may be said that the consonants were fixed in the time of Old High German.

2 On the other hand, the vowels were greatly modified. In unaccented syllables they were weakened to an unvoiced -*e*; this is certainly true for the final syllable, perhaps also for the pretonic. *Gilaubiu* > *geloube* is a good example of this.

3 In the accented syllables, a striking feature was the development of inflexion, particularly where the following syllable contained an *i* or a *j*: *almahtigon* > *almaehtigen* (and in the same way *schephaer* corresponding to the Old High German *scephâri*).

4 The weakening of final syllables naturally led to confusion in the inflective system. Another particularly clear example may be taken: that of the plural of the feminine substantive *zunge* (tongue). In Old High German it was declined in four cases: *zungûn*, *zungôno*, *zungôn*, *zungûn*. These three different forms were reduced to one: *zungen*.

5 Our text also reveals syntactical changes: the appearance of the personal pronoun (*iche geloube*), and of the article (*der erde*). This does not occur consistently, however. Compare the different treatment of *himels* (where the inflexion *s* is the sign of the genitive). Liturgical language, always extremely conservative, has kept the expression *Schöpfer Himmels und der Erde* right up to the present day.

The above text has been taken as an example. We could only arrive at the characteristics of Middle German by analysing numerous texts. We have concentrated on middle High German alone; there was also middle Low German, but the former has more bearing on the development of the language.

By the middle of the twelfth century a common literary language had come into being, that of court and lyric poetry. French influence is evident. There were many contacts between German and French knights during the Crusades, and also in their two countries. Hermann I, Landgrave of Thuringia, spent several months (in about 1160) at the court of Louis VII of France, before setting up his own brilliant court at the Wartburg. The German knights borrowed terms from the French: *Lanze, Turnei, Aventiure* (today Germanised into *Abenteuer*), *fein, stolz, falsch*.

The poets known as the 'Minnesingers' aimed at being understood by northerners and southerners alike. They eliminated the more definite dialectal forms. This is particularly apparent in their rhymes: Walter von der Vogelweide was Bavarian, and since the end of the eleventh century *î* had been diphthongised as *ei* in Bavaria, yet this poet rhymes *mîn, dîn* (today *mein, dein*) with *Konstantîn*. Even some Low German poets took part in this movement: Duke John of Brabant was still writing his love poems in High German in 1250. But the social basis of this *koinè* remained narrow and precarious.

In about 1227, Walter von der Vogelweide lamented: '*tanzen, lachen, singen, zergât mit sorgen gar*' (dancing, laughing, singing are supplanted by care). The splendid days of court society were over. The glory of the Empire was collapsing, power was dissolving everywhere: with the death of Frederick II in 1250 the great interregnum would begin.

The literary vitality of the dialects did not dwindle to a comparable degree. In about 1230, a little knight called Eike von Repgow described the customs of the Saxons in his *Sachsenspiegel*, written first in Latin, later in Low Saxon, mixed with turns of phrase in High Saxon (a Middle German dialect). This work had a considerable success: similar compilations were carried out, for instance for the Swabians.

Towards the end of the thirteenth century, a mystical school developed, especially among the Preaching Friars established along the Rhine. Its first great representative was Meister Eckhart (died 1327), probably an Alsatian, who taught at Strasbourg and Cologne. Other mystics, such as Mechtild von Magdeburg, came from different parts of the country. They made use of Latin to describe their intimate experiences of union with God, but were also prepared to write in German, and endowed their language with an abstract vocabulary which has remained alive to the present day: *begreifen*, *Verständnis*, *Einfluss*, *Zufall* are some of their creations.

At this time, too, charters and official documents began to be indited in German instead of in Latin. This did not always happen in the towns: the most important of them used scribes who wrote in Latin, the sons of bourgeois families went to the Church schools, and the earliest account-books that have come down to us (until 1400) were kept in Latin. The movement began among the landed gentry, who knew no Latin, and since they were not rich enough to employ scribes, had to write in German. These first charters in German appeared at the beginning of the thirteenth century: before the year 1299 about 2,500 of them are known, of which 2,200 were from the Rhineland, Switzerland, south Germany and Austria; most of them were the work of the landed gentry. Low Germany seems to have been much less productive; it was there, however, that the municipal laws were first transcribed in German: in 1227 at Braunschweig, as against 1276 at Augsburg. The situation was thus far from uniform. In 1235, Frederick II himself issued at Mainz, in German, his law concerning the public peace (*Land-friedengesetz*), and his example was widely followed. Thus, during the thirteenth century writings in German were no longer merely literary, and were increasing in number, but divergences of dialect seem to have been sanctified by this increase. If a writer wanted to be understood in about the year 1300, states Hugo von Trimberg, he had to make use of his *lantsprache*, or dialect. The true unification of German had yet to take place.

Before this happened, however, at least one linguistic group was sufficiently consolidated to pave the way for a language whose independence is recognised today – Dutch. The population of the Low Countries, as they were called, was made up of a good many elements: Frisians, Saxons and Franks. They led a relatively independent existence between the kingdom of France and the Empire, whose frontier traversed them. In particular, a remarkable wave of economic prosperity, based on efficient industrialisation, development of trade and agricultural improvements, made the whole of this region – first Flanders and then the other provinces – one of the most vital in Europe.

Various linguistic influences were felt in the Low Countries. Duke John of Brabant is said to have forced himself to write in High German. The towns of Flanders transcribed their documents in French: in 1298 a town charter providing for the annual appointment of aldermen was signed in French by important citizens with Flemish names. Yet works written in what might be called 'Middle Dutch' had already appeared. In Limburg, Heynrijck van Veldeke produced his *Eneit* in about 1170. In Brabant, a century later, Sister Hadewijck wrote letters and *Visions*, expressing ardent mysticism. In Flanders, Jacob van Maerlant (*c.* 1230–1300) made the transition from the literature of chivalry to bourgeois literature with truculent energy. These are noteworthy examples, but they are not isolated. And from the beginning of the fourteenth century the charters of Flemish towns were more and more often transcribed in Flemish.

Middle Dutch was not a unique dialect. Some of its dialectal characteristics were a sort of extension of Middle German, others of Low German. But it had its own independent existence. It was distinguished from High German by its consonantism, and from Low German by its vocalism: thus we notice the change from old Saxon *jung* to Middle Dutch *jonc*, the vocalisation of the *l* in groups such as *ald* (modern German *alt*) developing into *oud*, etc.

The wars of the fourteenth and sixteenth centuries were to give the Low Countries a separate political reality and sanctify the official existence of their language.

The results of the Iberian conquest

As with all other aspects of the life of the Iberian peninsula, linguistic evolution was dominated by the Reconquest. Of course it was only at a late date (in the twelfth century) that the *Reconquista* became a religious war. It had been for a long time an unambitious and rather confused struggle for possession of the best lands, in the course of which some of the Moslems became the allies of Christians against other Moslems, and vice versa. Nonetheless it was the Reconquest that ensured the predominance in Spain of the most original of Romance dialects. There is nothing here to remind us of the way Francian, a 'middle dialect', took the lead!

At the beginning of the eleventh century the greater part of the peninsula was under Moorish rule. Even for Christians among the indigenous population, Arabic was the language of culture (there was a monk called Mafomat, a distortion of Mahomet!). They spoke a language derived from Latin, a *romancium circa latinum* to borrow a contemporary description. It was even used in songs, thanks to which we have some acquaintance with it: for the Arab and Hebrew authors of *muwassahas* were in the habit of adding a four-lined stanza (*jarcha*) in the vulgar tongue to the end of these poems, which must have produced a strange effect. With a certain amount of difficulty (vowels have had to be supplied, as in Arabic), it has been possible to translate those *jarchas* that have been preserved. This dialectical body, which might be called Mozarabic, could have served as the basis of a national language, but for the Reconquest.

In the north, a series of more or less isolated and independent Christian states made up the nucleus of the Reconquest. Each of them developed a different spoken language, while their geographical situations and historical circumstances gave it its own physiognomy: from west to east they were Galicia, León, Navarre (whose central position seemed to destine it for a role of unification), Aragon embracing the central Pyrenees, and Catalonia. Like a sort of fortified border territory to León, Castile (or the country of castles, *castillos*) declared her independence in the tenth century and was the leader of the Reconquest; her dominion extended southwards in a strip cutting the peninsula into three and limiting the expansion of the other states. To the west, the Reconquest separated Galicia and formed Portugal. Eastwards, Aragon spent several decades in an obscure struggle to descend into the plain from the Pyrenees; she could only assist the Reconquest by an alliance with Catalonia, and it was the Catalans who spread south. The populations of Aragon, Navarre and León remained shut within their northern realms.

The Mozarabic dialect did not disappear without a struggle. A great many dialectal traces appear in texts of the twelfth and thirteenth centuries, for instance, in the Fuero (Charter) of Madrid before 1202. Its resistance also accounts for that part of the physiognomy of the Valencian dialect that distinguishes it from Catalan. In spite of everything, the inferiority of Mozarabic at the time of the Moorish rule deprived it of that prestige which might have imposed it on the conquerors.

It was Castilian that chiefly profited from its disappearance, and by the end of the thirteenth century the literary influence it had acquired enabled it to get the better of the dialect of León. Only Portuguese and Catalan resisted its powers of attraction.

The first appearance of the vulgar tongue was in the *Glosas Emilianenses* and *Silenses*, glosses composed during the tenth century in the monasteries of San Millán de la Cogolla and Silos, situated east and south-east of Burgos. These were sermons, litanies and other religious texts in Latin, with many words and sentences translated in the margin or between the lines, for the use of monks who found them hard to understand. These glosses show features of the dialects of both Navarre and Aragon; there are even two in Basque, which is explained by the proximity of the Basque country and the fact that some of the monks came from there. The similarities between these two documents suggest that their authors may have used the same glossary, which must have been owned by almost all the monasteries. Afterwards the standard of Latin teaching in the monasteries must have improved, as no more works of this sort are found.

It is in documents drawn up by notaries or secretaries of chancelleries that the vulgar tongue again reappears. As in the France of the *langue d'oc*, almost at the same period, the writers' poor knowledge of Latin led them to insert words from the popular language in their texts, and later to transcribe them entirely in the vulgar tongue. Menéndez Pidal was able to make a study of documents from León after the middle of the tenth century, from Castile after the beginning of the eleventh, and from Aragon after 1062. The same developments are found in Catalan in the eleventh century, and there is a text of Pallars entirely in Catalan, dating from between 1095 and 1110. We must not attach too much importance to exact dates, however, since they depend on the good or bad state of preservation of archives. Yet in Portuguese, this development definitely occurred later: the first known document in this language is a deed of partition of 1192, from the monastery of Vairão. By the thirteenth century the habit of inditing deeds in the vulgar tongue was making universal progress.

An oral literature undoubtedly preceded the first known literary texts in the 'rustic language'. In about 1150 the Latin Poem of Almeria speaks of Castilian as 'reverberating like a combination of trumpets and drums'. Dating from about the same time, probably 1140, is the only example that has been preserved of all this epic literature (except for a few fragments): the *Cantar de mio Cid*, inspired by the adventures of Rodrigo Diaz de Vivar, a nobleman who had been outlawed by the King of Castile, and whose career ended with the conquest of the kingdom of Valencia. The 3,735 lines of this poem (the first page has been lost) have reached us through a thirteenth-century copy, in which the original may have been altered to some extent. It must have been composed either near Burgos and Vivar, or farther south near Medinaceli, perhaps by two authors.

Castilian appeared next in a variety of religious texts, and in the thirteenth century its suitability as a literary language was definitely established: King Alfonso x, the Learned, (who reigned from 1252 to 1284) was responsible for the triumph of Castilian prose. He surrounded himself with lawyers and scholars, and commissioned juridical works (particularly the Code known as the *Siete Partidas* because it was composed in seven sections), as well as histories (the *Primera Crónica General de España* and the *General Estoria Universal*) and scientific treatises (*Saber de Astronomia, Lapidario*). Many of these were merely translations or adaptations from Latin.

However, Alfonso x, who was also a poet, wrote his *Canticles of the Virgin* in Portuguese still strongly tinged with Galician. The melancholy character of the race that spoke this language, and its sweet, soft sound, may explain why this thirteenth-century lyric poem in Portuguese had such a success even outside the national frontiers. It was agreed at the time that Portuguese was more suitable for lyric poetry, and Castilian for epics and history.

The literary history of Catalan seems to have been rather different. The success of the Occitan poetry written at the court of Alfonso the Chaste, King of Aragon and Count of Barcelona, explains why Catalan first made its appearance in prose: the first work was a collection of sermons, written in a hand that must date at least from the end of the twelfth century, the *Homilies d'Organya*. This text was preserved in the village of that name, in the high valley of the river Segre; one may suppose that it was not the only one of its day. Literary Catalan came into its own during the thirteenth century, under the patronage of King Jaime 1 the Conqueror (reigned from 1213 to 1276), who made his Chancellery use

Catalan, and himself collaborated in the great chronicle of his reign, *Llibre dels Feyts del rei En Jacme*. This was the beginning of an admirable flowering of historical works in Catalan, at the same time that Ramon Llull (*c.* 1233–1315) was writing philosophical and scientific works.

The researches into these documents undertaken by Menéndez Pidal and his pupils enable us to follow the development of the 'Spanish' language in a particularly interesting manner, from the pre-literary stage of the first documents until norms gradually became fixed. At first the differences in the scripts do not only reveal orthographic uncertainty, but attempts to translate an evolving pronunciation as accurately as possible. Thus, documents from León write the word for territory: *territorio, terretorio, terridorio, territurio, terreturio, terredurio, terridurio*, etc.

Even during this uncivilised period, the influence of Latin was considerable: it was not confined to the vocabulary, as happened later; numerous phonetic and morphologic 'cultisms' can be noticed where the scribe has tried to return to what he believes was the original Latin. They sometimes even result in hyper-corrections, which are commonest in an ignorant environment. Thus, in applying the rule by which the voiced consonant in Romance often corresponds to an unvoiced consonant in Latin, the scribe might write *intecro* or *conticuos*, whereas in both these cases the Latin consonant was in fact voiced: *integro* (entire), *contiguos* (contiguous)!

We see the essential feature of a pre-literary period emerging: it is not the absence of norms, but the co-existence of several norms at war among themselves. The struggle lasted a very long time, and linguists may get an impression of extreme confusion, or even conclude that every word has its separate history, and distrust phonetic or morphological laws. A collective development was, however, really going on. Menéndez Pidal used the image of leaves falling onto the surface of a stream; all were carried along by it, even if the interplay of currents and obstacles hurried some along, delayed others and left the fate of yet others uncertain.

After this time, literary influences took effect in a very erratic manner. Epic poetry, seeking after grandeur and strangeness, repeated ritual formulas (attached to their hero), and made use of a carefully chosen archaic vocabulary. Dialectic poetry, in its effort to familiarise the hearer with difficult subjects, had recourse to concrete terms, multiplied its images, and showed a fondness for diminutives, but was in general conformist as to syntax and morphology.

Alfonso x's influence also imposed norms on prose writing, which had hitherto kept to a monotonous syntactic simplicity. One development stands out clearly from the immense body of work accomplished at the king's court. The oldest part of the *Crónica General* reveals certain irregularities: the final *e* is often dropped (*trist*, *pued*), and separate words are combined. These anomalies vanished afterwards; with a few exceptions, the final *e* was re-established and has been kept until the present day. The king intervened in person: in 1276 he went through the text of the *Book of the Eighth Sphere*, written by his collaborators, eliminating irregularities, clumsiness and repetitions. In this way he arrived at a *castellano drecho* (correct, pure Castilian), corresponding on the whole with the usage of Burgos, but with certain concessions to Toledo and León. The written language was thus fixed. Syntax achieved remarkable flexibility of expression, and the vocabulary was enriched by borrowing scientific terms and also by exploiting the possibilities of the language.

The characteristics of Castilian thus emerged with increasing clearness, and can be summarised as follows:

The vocalic system was a peculiarly simple one, founded on the five vowels of classical Latin; the diphthongs *ai* and *au* were reduced to *e* (as we have seen) or *o* (*auru(m)* > *oro*). It was remarkable that Castilian tended to create diphthongs and then eliminate them. The consonantal system evolved considerably, on the other hand: *b* and *v* soon became confused; the unvoiced intervocalic explosives of Latin were now voiced; *g* developed into *dj* and then the yod before an accented *e* or *i* (*generum > yerno*), and disappeared before unstressed *e* or *i* (*germanum > hermano*). The *l* was palatalised in groups of consonants, giving *clavem > llave* in an initial position, and the sound *dz* in the interior of a word, which was to evolve towards *j* (*foliam > hoja*). But the most important change was that of initial *f* to *h* (*fabulare > hablar*, to speak; *filium > hijo*, son), found once more in Gascon. This phenomenon has taxed the intelligence of linguists.

Menéndez Pidal has expounded his reasons for placing it very early. Toponyms of the eleventh century already show signs of it. Study of the scripts of the twelfth to fourteenth centuries shows a progressive generalisation of the *h* with a hyper-corrective tendency due to a reaction against a popular phenomenon. Menéndez Pidal concludes that we have to do with the influence of a very ancient substratum, Basque or Iberian. Other linguists have shown that this phenomenon is not general in Basque, but occurs in other dialects. John Orr infers a rustic substratum under Etruscan influence. At all events, one may suppose that the influence of the substratum was not absolute, and that it was mainly expressed by choice between co-existing forms. And in some cases it allowed the alternative to remain, *festa > fiesta* (whereas Gascon had *histo*).

We can pass more rapidly over the subjects of morphology and syntax, whose evolution was fairly simple, and even of vocabulary, in which the importance of borrowings from Arabic has already been stressed. It only remains to indicate French influence, which can be largely explained by pilgrimages to Santiago de Compostela, French participation in the *Reconquista*, and the re-population of the Iberian peninsula. Besides which, Castilian shares some features with Portuguese and Catalan.

There were dialectal zones in Portugal: numerous differences distinguished the spoken language of Galicia in the north from that of the central zone. But the distinction did not become clear until the fourteenth century, and it was later still that central Portuguese, used by many great writers, triumphed as the language of literature. In any case, thirteenth-century texts reveal the chief characteristics of modern Portuguese.

The development of vocalism was simple: we do not even find diphthongisation of the accented vowels, as in Castilian, but *nossa* instead of cast. *nuestra* (our), *festa* for cast. *fiesta* (festivity). Of the unvoiced final vowels, only *e* was dropped, and *a* and *o* were kept. The most original feature was the nasalisation of a great many vowels, usually open and tonic, which the scribes took trouble to express, writing *partiçoens*, but *divisoes* (today these are indicated by the sign *õe*, *ão*). The development of consonants was also simple, unlike that of Castilian. The evolution of initial groups of consonants will be noted, such as *cl-*, *pl- > ch-* (*clamare > chamar*, to call; *plenum > cheio*, full); on the other hand the palatalisation of the initial *c-* was hardly ever seen except in words of French origin (*chefe*). In the interior of words, intervocalic *c* ended as *ts* (*placere > prazer*, pleasure), *g* fused with *e* or *i* following it (*cogitare > cuidar*, think), *l* disappeared (*dolor > dor*, pain), *n* nasalised the preceding vowel and was dropped (*manum > mao*, hand). But most Latin consonants were preserved. As for morphology, the preservation of the Latin subjunctive imperfect may be noted in the form of the personal infinitive. The vocabulary was strongly affected by French influence.

Even someone ignorant of the Catalan language is struck by the large number of consonants in relation to vowels. This 'consonantism' of Catalan is explained by the way both consonants and vowels have developed from Latin.

As for vowels, all post-tonics except *a* disappeared, and even *a* was in fact unvoiced, much like the silent *e* in French; diphthongs were few, none were spontaneous (*proba* > *prova*, cf. cast. *prueba*, proof), and many conditioned diphthongs quickly evolved into simple vowels (*noctem* > *nit*, cf. port. *noite*, arag. *nueyt*).

Nonetheless, Catalan possesses one true diphthong, *au* or *eu*, which can be formed in several ways (*videre* > *veure*). As for consonants, Latin sounds were well preserved: the initial groups *cl-*, *fl*, *pl-* remaining; initial *l-* was often palatalised (*lactem* > *llet*). The final *n* was dropped, but without nasalising the preceding vowel as in Portuguese. A very curious feature was the development of the periphrastic perfect (*vaig cantar*, I sang) which appeared in the fourteenth century, probably at first with a future significance, but ending as the narrative present, referring to the past.

Thus the various languages of the Iberian peninsula diverged. In spite of geographical proximity and similar historical destinies, each developed – as well as numerous traits in common – an original character which has been preserved until the present day, in spite of the influence exerted by Castilian from the fifteenth century onwards.

Italy: the power of poetry

Italy is the native land of Latin. Charlemagne acquired the first masters of his Renaissance from Italy, even before he was provided by others more brilliant still from the Anglo-Saxon countries. Education remained relatively developed and the traditions of legal writing were uninterrupted. Vippone di Borgogna reproached the Germans for failing to realise that other people besides the clergy could be educated, and Raoul Glaber recognised that it was characteristic of the Italians to devote themselves to grammar above all the other 'arts'. It was natural to write in Latin, even in practical life; as late as 1266, at Genoa, a deed executed by a notary made it clear that merchants learned Latin at that time.

However, the language of daily conversation was diverging from ancient Latin, though the Italians were slow to realise the fact. One might say that there had been a long period of unconscious bilingualism. Gregory v's epitaph, quoted on page 101, is an isolated piece of evidence. In the twelfth century, recommendations were issued which took into account the general ignorance of Latin: for instance, a bishop of Catania decreed that if an adult catechumen did not know his letters (that is to say Latin), he should recite the baptismal formula *vulgariter*. Such incidents increased later, and in 1246 the Statutes of Bologna insisted that candidates for notaryships should give proof of their ability to read to the public in the vulgar tongue the deeds they had drawn up themselves in Latin.

Written Italian made a somewhat stealthy entrance onto the scene. The earliest traces of it are found in the *Proceedings of Monte Cassino*, where, between 900 and 963, rights of ownership over certain lands were made public by witnesses who affirmed them in the vulgar tongue: a similar procedure to that which had resulted in the Strasbourg Oaths. Certain characteristic features, such as the dropping of the final consonant, appeared in this text. After this, we must wait until the end of the eleventh century for other humble documents to come to light, and they did not become numerous until the twelfth century. Most of these texts are markedly dialectal in character. For a long time partition was practically complete: everything of general interest was written in Latin: the vulgar tongue had merely local value and only appeared in the form of dialect. Because of this, some linguists have questioned whether the Italian language was spoken before the thirteenth century.

The barriers of dialect had to be surmounted in the case of political, economic or religious relations between towns or regions. But Italy suffered more than any other European country from a disastrous lack of political unity. The lighthouse of imperial power did not shine for her as for Germany: the emperor was a stranger, fought against in the north, violently opposed by the papacy, and recognised late (and temporarily) in the south. Centres of attraction were manifold: there was remarkable economic prosperity in the great cities of the north and Tuscany; the position achieved by the university of Bologna was unequalled and it attracted students from all over Europe; Rome was the religious centre of Christianity; only the south was subjected to true monarchy, that of the Norman kings of Sicily, who were succeeded by the brilliant reign of Frederick II of Hohenstaufen, and afterwards by the Angevins. This was not a situation which favoured unification of the vulgar tongue, nor even its emancipation.

It was in literature, and first of all in poetry, that these aims were realised. We are faced here with the problem of the influence of French literature, in the *langue d'oïl* and Occitan, both of which had great success. In the twelfth century a Bolognese jurist spoke of the blind men who sang of the adventures of Sire Roland and Oliver in his town. Several works written in a hybrid Franco-Italian testified to this new fashion in their own way. French was spoken at the Norman court of Sicily, and a Sicilian count gave his ignorance of the language as an excuse for refusing the regency (in 1166). Lyric poetry in the *langue d'oc* also acquired great prestige in the twelfth century, and in the thirteenth this was reinforced by the arrival in Italy of troubadours fleeing from the Albigensian Crusade. The poet Sordello of Mantua composed *cansos* and *sirventes* in that language; he must, it is true, have spent some twenty years in Provence, but he was not the only one of his kind. In a sense the vogue for French literature delayed the awakening of Italian literature.

Yet it also encouraged it, if only by the fact that it was an example of a literature in the vulgar tongue. If others had produced such works, could not Italy herself do so? In about 1200 the first poems in various Italian dialects appeared. Soon what was known as the 'Sicilian School' flowered, a collection of twenty-nine poets of different origins, grouped round Frederick ii, writing lyric poetry in the style of the troubadours. The language they wrote in seems to have been a *koinè*: characteristics borrowed from continental dialects, Tuscan in particular, give the impression that an effort was being made to create a common language, over and above the dialects. But this impression may be false, resulting from a subsequent 'Tuscanisation' of these poems, which were very possibly originally written in *illustre* Sicilian; that is to say, a refined and elegant form of the local dialect. At all events, this Sicilian poetry had an immense and immediate success on the continent, where it was taken up by the so-called 'Siculo-Tuscans', such as Guittone d'Arezzo and later the poets of the 'stil nuovo', such as Guinicelli. Certain of its original characteristics survived this form of transference: thus Sicilian only possessed five vowels, and did not distinguish between open and closed *o*, or open and shut *e*; the Tuscans, on the other hand, did make these distinctions, but allowed themselves the licence of rhyming closed and open *o* and *e*, and even closed *o* with *u*, and closed *e* with *i*.

Other poetical forms spread freely: Francis of Assisi and Jacopone da Todi founded an Umbrian school of more popular religious poetry, such as canticles and lauds; in northern Italy from Genoa to Cremona and Verona, religious and dialectic versification flourished.

Prose followed suit. In the thirteenth-century texts relating to practical matters increased in number: account-books, business letters, contracts and inscriptions. It has been possible to publish two volumes of those from Florence alone. Narrative prose took the form of chronicles or popularisations. In northern and central Italy, it became the custom for a *podestà* or leader to deliver speeches in public, and the University of Bologna produced a Rhetoric in the vulgar tongue for their use. But the linguistic habits of prose differed from those of poetry. Diphthongisation did not follow the same rules, for one thing: Guittone – and Dante after him – used to write *novo* in poetry and *nuovo* in prose.

Most of these writings in poetry and prose showed dialectal characteristics, in spite of the efforts they made to be widely understood. This was chiefly noticeable in their orthography and phonetics. Thus in west Tuscan, the group *th* was equivalent to *z* (*vethosa* for *vezzosa*, graceful), while a Florentine would write *cz* or *tz*. The reduction of *uo* to *u* (*furi* for *fuòri*, outside) was Umbrian, and was also found at Arezzo, close by. The Sardinian and Piedmontese dialects represented two extremes of divergence. From reading thirteenth-century authors one gets the impression that they thought of these dialects as separate languages: does not Salimbene praise a certain Friar Barnabas, in about 1250, for 'speaking French, Tuscan and Lombard so well'?

However, by the thirteenth century, the Italian language really existed, and most of the features it was to preserve had already definitely appeared. Its phonetics were rather conservative, especially as to vowels, which were the same as those of Latin. Diphthongisation was one of the aspects that varied most from one dialect to another. There were few developments of the form *pedem > piede*, *focum > fuoco*. Some diphthongs came from the palatalisation of *l* after a consonant (*plus > più*), others from the dropping of a final *s* (*pos(t) > poi*). As for consonants, there was more doubling than in Latin, which already had *secco* and *anno*, but not *femmina*, *cammino*; this often resulted from assimilation (*factum > fatto*), occasionally even from false etymology (*la rettorica* attributed to *rectores*!). Affricates were numerous:

this proliferation resulted from the evolution of internal groups, of which the second element was a yod, thus *pretium > prezzo*, *hodie > oggi*. The complete elimination of final consonants happened very soon, and it was unconsciously assumed that every word must end in a vowel. In morphology, it will be noticed that Latin declensions disappeared, except for a few scholarly usages. The syntactical physiognomy of Italian had been clearly defined by the thirteenth century. Constructions had been invented which made it useless to grammaticise *uomo*, as happened to French *on* or German *man*.

The vocabulary seems to have been considerably enriched before the end of the thirteenth century. Because of its closeness to Latin, Italian easily absorbed Latinisms into the popular language as well as into the vocabulary of scholarship. Nevertheless a definite resistance was set up, and some terms were not accepted until later: for instance *facile* in opposition to *agevole*, *esèrcito* to *oste* (of Germanic origin). Otherwise, the sources of Italian were extremely varied, and none of them predominated as Frankish had done in Gaul or Arabic in the Iberian peninsula. A great many Gallicisms were introduced up to the end of the thirteenth century: they were mainly concerned with chivalry (*cavaliere*, *scudiere*, *gonfalone*), travel (*viaggio*, *ostello*), and the economy. Many terms came from literature (*avventura*, *pensiero*). Occitan was an equally rich mine, and appeared in suffixes like *-aggio*, from the Provençal *-atge* (*coraggio*). It is not, however, always easy to distinguish words of French and Occitan origin. There were also Arabisms. But, in spite of the fact that Italy was part of the Empire, borrowings from Germanic were rare, the most famous being provided by the names of the Guelphs and the Ghibellines.

The thirteenth century closed with the great figure of Dante. It was typical of Italy for an outstanding personality to have such an extraordinary influence on linguistics as well as on literature. Did Dante really deserve the description so often applied to him, of 'father of the Italian language'? Strictly speaking, no: our exposition has stressed the existence of Italian before Dante's time. Nevertheless the influence of his ideas as well as of his own work was immense.

The ideas expressed by Dante in his treatise *De vulgari eloquentia*, written about 1303, concern a wider sphere than Italy alone, and deserve to be examined separately (pages 149–52). But it is impossible to pass over in silence Dante's detailed description of the Italian dialects. He distinguished between at least fourteen dialectal groups, and considered which of them were the basis for the literary language, or *volgare illustre*, that he used himself. If he is hard on such dialects as Roman, Milanese and Sardinian, he also dismisses Bolognese in spite of its obvious qualities, Tuscan in spite of the arrogant claims of those who spoke it, and Sicilian in spite of the fame of Frederick II's court. He came to the conclusion that the *volgare illustre* transcended all dialects, while extracting something from each. Thus Dante set aside his pride in his own town, in favour of the notion of a common and truly Italian language. His strong interest in linguistics, as well as his praise of the common vulgar tongue, sanctioned earlier developments and gave them a new impetus.

Again, in such different works as the earliest lyrics and the *Divine Comedy*, Dante displayed the expressive possibilities of this language with incomparable skill. He made a great many stylistic and prosodic discoveries, and was clearly influenced by the great Latin writers. His grammar and vocabulary were far from exclusively Florentine. He used various forms according to the requirements of rhythm and rhyme – for instance *diceva* or *dicea*, *lasciare* or *lassare*, *re* or *rege*, *specchio*, *speglio* or *speculo* (mirror). He welcomed a great number of Florentine words, some of them popular, but he also borrowed from the vocabularies of other dialects when they already had the sanction of literary use.

Dante's influence was in fact enormous. It was thanks to him that the rather artificial *koinè* he had assembled was absorbed into a permanent literary tradition. This was probably also due to a closer rapprochement than in other countries between the language of literature and scholarship and the popular language; social evolution presumably followed a different course. At all events, while in other countries such as southern France or Germany the *koinè* realised by the poetry of chivalry vanished with the decline of the social class that had supported it, in Italy the literary tradition survived, above the vigorous and productive dialects and proudly aware of its linguistic originality.

Latin

While the Romance languages were crystallising and assuming new importance, medieval Latin was also reaching its apogee. Now was the time of fusion and equilibrium between its constituent elements: the classical tradition, the inspiration of Christianity and the influence of the vulgar tongues. The proportion between these elements varied from one author to another, and neologisms of vulgar origin were not always the same. In spite of this, medieval Latin led an independent life, it was truly the 'autonomous and free instrument of thought',[8] and it offered the incomparable advantages of a cultured language common to the whole of Europe.

It was learned in the schools, generally with the help of the grammars of Priscian and Donat. The soundness of the teaching was measurable by the quality of the results: in the whole body of twelfth- and thirteenth-century texts, including documents and works of literature, inflexion, declensions and conjugations were normally used correctly, agreements were respected, the vocabulary was satisfyingly rich, and the syntax agreeably easy and sometimes even elegant. Of course, it must not be supposed that these qualities were found in all those whose duties involved the use of Latin, in the lower ranks of the clergy in particular. Episcopal visits were often edifying, and among others there is a well-known story of a poor parish priest who, when questioned about one of the first sentences in the Mass (*Te igitur clementissime Pater supplices rogamus ac petimus*: therefore we beg and pray you, oh most merciful Father), admitted that he could not translate the word *clementissime*, nor say what was the grammatical case of *te*. When asked 'What word governs it?' he replied: '*Pater*, because the Father governs all things'. But even in our own era of general education, is the knowledge of grammar much above this level? At the opposite end of the scale, we have some idea of the high quality attained by the best Latin teaching. An Englishman, John of Salisbury, described the education he received at the episcopal school of Chartres about the middle of the twelfth century: Bernard de Chartres read aloud Latin authors, carefully pointing out current expressions, stylistic ornaments and the various grammatical figures, and insisting on the proper use of terms. After which he advised his pupils not to 'cover themselves with another man's garment so as to make their own work more brilliant', and this denunciation of plagiarism implied that classical Latin must not be slavishly copied – a new and living Latin must be created.

This aspiration was realised by Latin literature of the twelfth century. A man so hostile to luxury and useless embellishments as Bernard de Clairvaux, nevertheless wrote in a prose that was not only polished, but strengthened by the use of rhythm, rhyme and alliterations, which naturally expressed his mystical exaltation. The letters of Abelard and Heloise surprise us so much by their purity and elegance that we are tempted, in the face of all the evidence, to see these cries from the heart (and body) as an academic exercise. Thus education was not everything, habit had become second nature and was no longer divided from first nature. With whatever emotion we may greet the first works written in a vulgar tongue, it must be said that the Latin literature of the twelfth century stands in the highest rank for quality and quantity, that it was written in a language that had proved capable of evolution, and that it bears comparison with many masterpieces of classical antiquity.

But the balance gradually shifted during the thirteenth century, reflecting considerable social developments. The growth of social categories such as the landed gentry and bourgeoisie, and their acquisition of a culture which owed little to Latin, enlarged the audience for national literature. The increased number of universities, translations of Aristotle and other ancient authors, made Latin a predominantly scholarly language. Grammar was now merely a practical art. Above all, Latin became the 'technical language of abstract thought',[9] served by a precision, a delicacy of expression and a richness of vocabulary which was only very gradually to be equalled by the new languages.

The end of the thirteenth century ushered in a new Europe.

HOW IS IT possible to describe the linguistic evolution of Europe in the fourteenth and fifteenth centuries without first conjuring up the figure of Dante? Dante does not belong only to Italy, although his work made a potent contribution to the birth of Italian literature. Although he never gave definitive shape to his treatise *De vulgari eloquentia*, whose first draft was made about 1303, this little work is both revealing of the road travelled in Europe in the thirteenth century, and prophetically significant, thanks to the author's astonishing personality.

Dante searched for the origins of the common literary language used by Italian poets, which he called the '*volgare illustre*'. First of all, what was this 'vulgar eloquence'? In opposition to grammar (Latin) as taught in the schools, it was, he said, what each of us learnt by imitating our nurse, without consciously following any rule – the mother tongue in fact. Of the two, it was far the noblest: it was the earliest to be used by human beings; although diverse, it was by nature common to all, for every man possessed a mother tongue; it was more natural than the studied, artificial language of 'grammar'.

What then was the origin of language? Dante's concept of God's immateriality was much too definite for him to admit that He had to use a particular language to make His wishes plain. Man was the first to speak, and his first word must have been 'God' in Hebrew. Hebrew was the unique primitive language, Dante agreed, just as he connected linguistic plurality with the episode of Babel. During the dispersal that followed it, three groups came to populate Europe:

> Whether these men arrived there as strangers or were returning to Europe as natives, they brought with them three languages; amongst them, some took the southern part, and others the northern part of Europe for their own; the third group, which we now call the Greeks, settled partly in Europe and partly in Asia.

More precisely, Dante designated these groups by the word they used as an affirmative. *Jo*, said the men of the north. The south-western group (Latin) were themselves divided: 'for some of them affirm by saying *oc* (Occitan), others by saying *oïl* (French) and others by saying *si*' (Italian and the Iberian languages).

Next Dante concentrated his attention on Italy. He was struck by the diversity of its spoken languages, noticeable from one town to another, and even 'more astounding still, between the inhabitants of the same city, for instance, in Bologna, those of San Felice and those of the Strada Maggiore'. This diversity was due to man himself 'the most unstable and variable of animals', and was bound up with his historical evolution, for

> we seem much further away from the first inhabitants of our own town than from our contemporaries in distant lands. I will go so far as to say, that if the ancient people of Pavia could return to life, they would converse with the modern inhabitants of that town in a different, or several different languages.

Among all this variety Dante succeeded in distinguishing

fourteen dialectal groups, and he studied their contributions to the '*volgare illustre*' in turn (cf. page 145).

What do we find most remarkable in all this? We need not praise Dante extravagantly for having been aware of the kinship between languages: this was after all based on the scheme set out in Genesis, to which he remained faithful. From similar assumptions, others before him had made comments that were at least as penetrating. As early as 1194, Giraldus de Barri (Giraldus Cambrensis), noted in his *Description of the country of Wales* (1, 15) 'that nearly all words in the Breton language have a word corresponding to them in Greek or Latin'. He certainly exaggerated: this does not prevent seven out of fourteen examples given by Giraldus being perfectly correct.

The classification of European languages in three groups (Greek, Germanic and Latin, subdivided into the Romance languages) deserves the attention it aroused. Yet Dante was not the first to follow this path. Before him, the great Ximenes de Rada, Archbishop of Toledo, had presented an even completer linguistic picture of Europe in his *De rebus Hispaniae*, written before 1243. Ximenez had a better knowledge of eastern Europe; he clearly distinguished the Greeks from the Bulgarians and Hungarians, traced the limits of the Slavonic group (only omitting the Russians), made plain the subdivisions in the Germanic group, and showed some knowledge of Gaelic and Basque. Dante had not travelled so widely as he had, nor received such a rich university education. On the other hand, for exactness and precision, there is nothing to compare with Dante's description of Italy.

We are at least as much indebted to him for having so vehemently proclaimed the outstanding importance of the vulgar tongue. It was the heritage of at least two centuries of literary flowering. In Dante's day, the greatest works of literature were written in the vulgar tongue, and his contribution was more outstanding than any. There was no going back on this achievement in spite of the humanist crisis.

Dante's realisation that languages were evolving was more original still, even if he was not really able to analyse the causes. That was a task that would not be carried out for several centuries, despite the beginnings of linguistic analysis in the fourteenth and fifteenth centuries.

Latin and the vulgar tongues

While Dante was proclaiming the eminence and dignity of the vulgar tongues, their sphere of use was ceaselessly being extended in Italy, as elsewhere.

This primarily applied to documents concerned with practical life. In Italy, statutes were more frequently written in Italian; in Florence, in 1356, Sir Andrea Lancia was charged with the task of vulgarising all those of the Republic within a year, for the use of citizens. Latin put up more resistance in the sphere of public correspondence: the chancelleries were accustomed to it. However, in the fifteenth century, Italian began to oust it: at Milan, Filippo Maria Visconti gave it definite support; similar progress was noted at Ferrara, where the disadvantages of Latin were illustrated by an anecdote. The Duke wrote to a neighbouring podestà at Modena to send him a falcon tied in a sack (*capias accipitrem et mitte nobis ligatum in sacculo ne aufugiat*), but the recipient failed to understand, and sent the archpriest instead of the bird that had been asked for! In Germany, the chancelleries gradually began substituting German for Latin in the middle of the thirteenth century. In the British Isles, the English language was making definite progress, although concealed by the competition of French; a great many private letters were still being written in Latin, but this stopped in about 1450. In France, the Royal Chancellery was using French more and more: still uncommon under Louis ix and Philippe iii, it was currently used in the fourteenth century, in the countries of the *langue d'oil* at least, and particularly by the local authorities in the towns. Speeches in parliament were nearly always in French. Decrees were written in Latin, it is true, in order to be understood throughout the country, including the region of the *langue d'oc*. But in 1336 the head of a tribunal advised the use of 'crude Latin, the friend of the laity' (*latinum grossum pro laicis amicum*): he meant by this a text modelled on French, but tricked out in Latin terminations, which would be very ridiculous to our eyes. Everywhere, Latin was retiring into what were to be its traditional refuges: the Church, official tribunals and the universities.

The success of the vulgar tongues in the domain of literature was nothing new. But they triumphed in certain forms that had hitherto been reserved for Latin. Encouraged by Dante, Boccaccio composed an epic in Italian, the *Teseida*. On the whole, social evolution and progress due to education and curiosity inspired the growth of a didactic literature in the vulgar tongues. This included many translations and embraced almost all special subjects. Livy was translated into Italian by Boccaccio, and into French by Bersuire. Philosophy was tackled, Dante having declared the aptitude of the vulgar tongues for this subject: in France, the translation of Aristotle's works was entrusted by Charles v to Nicole Oresme. Scientific works on medicine, surgery and agronomy multiplied. Religious literature was considerably enriched: Wycliffe's translation of the Bible into English (1384); in German, the works of the fourteenth-century mystics (Eckhart, Suso, Tauler); in French, theological treatises by Gerson (1363–1429) are merely beacons indicating an enormous production which undoubtedly corresponded to a deepening of religious life, and contained the germs of the disputes of the Reformation.

In translation, as with the composition of original works, a whole technical, philosophical and scientific vocabulary had to be created, which often followed Latin with more or less complete servility. Wycliffe's Bible contains a great many words such as 'generation', 'persecution', which did not figure in the Old English version. When translating Pliny, Landino excused himself:

> Non so come interpreti 'seminario' et 'arbusta', item 'ablaqueare' et 'interlucare', se non per circonlocutione o per il medesimo vocabolo.

> (I don't know how to render 'seminario' and 'arbusta', or 'ablaqueare' and 'interlucare', but by means of circumlocution, or by the word itself.)

Out of respect or idleness, many French translators declared that they could find no words except those adapted in some sort from the Latin model. Everywhere, an enormous mass of often necessary Latinisms was pouring into the vulgar tongues, and reinforcing their 'Latinity'. These growing-pains were inevitable, but they were accompanied by the disputations of the humanists.

Even those writers who made a brilliant contribution to literature in the vulgar tongue, retained a special familiarity with Latin, and a sort of reverence for this clerical language. The annotations Petrarch scribbled on his manuscripts, as though commenting on the rhymes, were in Latin: *hic non placet, dic aliter* (this does not fit, say it another way). Much more serious than this professional attachment was the movement to admire ancient writers – Cicero in particular – which developed in Italy in the fourteenth century. It was the glorification of the secular life, their specifically humanist ideals that were prized. But the classical purity of their style was all the more impressive because of the fact that there had been no outstanding work written in Latin since the twelfth century. In Florence, Coluccio Salutati introduced the antique style in the Chancellery correspondence, and he reproached another writer for writing 'like a monk'. In the same way, Lorenzo Valla criticised the Latin of philosophers. The vulgar tongues

had had it all their own way against the bastard Latin of the
thirteenth century. Things were very different when they were
faced with the revival of classical Latin. Dante himself found
no favour in the eyes of the humanists. He would have been
superior to the Greeks and Latins, said Salutati, if only he had
written in Latin. Niccoli reproached him for being a sort of
demagogue: 'That is why, Coluccio, I would keep your poet
away from the advice of scholars, and leave him with belt-
makers, bakers, and others of that sort.'

Sooner or later, with more or less intensity, the controversy
began in every European country. In France, it was in about
1400 that humanists such as Jean de Montreuil, Gontier Col
and Nicolas de Clamanges, encouraged by their travels in Italy
or to Avignon, read the writers of antiquity, and 'tasted and
savoured' their thoughts enthusiastically; the troubles of the
period prevented their carrying these impulses far: the first two
perished as victims of the Burgundian reaction in 1418. In
England, enthusiasm for humanism was manifested in the
persistence of the habit of writing private letters in Latin. In
Spain, links with Italy were strengthened by the conquest of
the kingdom of Naples (1442); a certain Juan de Mena went so
far as to describe the Iliad as a 'blessed and seraphic work'.

This crisis had profound effects everywhere on literature in
the vulgar tongue. In Italy, in the century separating the death
of Boccaccio (1375) from the beginning of printing (1470)
there was not a single great writer in Italian. As soon as a writer
of literary talent appeared, he tended to express himself in
Latin. Left to itself, the vulgar tongue welcomed all new forms
indiscriminately: this was particularly true of Tuscan. In Spain,
an examination of Castilian reveals, besides an invasion by a
whole Latin vocabulary, clumsy use of Latin turns of phrase
and usage: the adjective separated from the substantive (*pocos
hallo que de las mías se paguen obras*. Enrique de Villena – I find
few who like my works); the introduction of constructions
using the infinitive (*honestidad e contenencia non es dubda ser muy*

grandes e escogidas virtudes – there is no doubt that honesty and continence are very great and distinguished virtues).

The weaknesses of this reaction were evident at the social as well as the linguistic level. It was the expression of an aristocratic ideal, necessarily confined to small 'elites'. The humanists soon learned to extend and deepen their ideal. One of the greatest of them, the Florentine writer and architect Leon Battista Alberti (1404–72), out of his conviction that the vulgar tongue could express the noblest concepts, organised, with the support of Piero de' Medici, the competition of the *Certame coronario*: on 22 October 1441, eight competitors met in the church of Santa Maria dei Fiori, and extolled true friendship in Italian. The results were mediocre, and the silver crown was not even bestowed. Summer may not have been heralded by a swallow, but it did arrive in due course. The merits of the *toscana lingua* were fully celebrated by Lorenzo de' Medici in about 1476, whether by sending Frederick of Aragon a selection of lyrical works, or by praising the richness, sweetness and harmony of the language that was *commune a tutta Italia*. In Spain, while Antonio de Nebrija was organising the serious study of the Greek and Latin writers of antiquity, the blind admiration and the affectation of the early days vanished. 'Common humanism' triumphed everywhere. And in the sixteenth century, Spenser was able to reconcile and grade at the same time passions that were not really contradictory:

'I love Rome, but London better. I favour Italie, but England more. I honor the Latin, but I worship the English.'

The vulgar tongues thus definitely triumphed over Latin. But which vulgar tongues?

Language and nation

At the beginning of the fourteenth century, the linguistic geography of Europe still seems to have been confused. In some places, no real unification of dialectal groups that were very much alive had yet taken place. In others, it was incomplete, or else several vulgar tongues were at war within the same nation. This picture was taking shape and becoming simpler.

It was in England that developments were probably the clearest. At the end of the thirteenth century, Robert of Gloucester deplored (with a certain amount of exaggeration) that there was no country 'that holdeth not to its own speech, save England only'. The form of trilingualism in operation there, at least at the 'elite' level, has already been described. But whereas Latin was confined to religious and scholarly circles, as elsewhere, the retreat of French became headlong during the fourteenth century. It was above all the hatred bred by the Hundred Years War that widened the breach. English was introduced into the schools in 1349. In 1362 Parliament was opened in English. Henry IV spoke in English when he claimed the Crown from the unfortunate Richard II (1399). In 1413 English became the official language of the Court. Certain traditional usages of French were preserved; thus it did not become obligatory to speak English in the courts of justice until the eighteenth century. Such oddities were merely put up with: 'for the mooste quantyte of the people understonde not latyn ne frensshe in this noble royaume of England', as Caxton said.

At the same time written English was being standardised throughout the British Isles. England provides a convenient example of dialectal cartography. By a certain simplification we arrive at five dialects, spoken in the north, the east and west midlands, the south and Kent. 'Standard English' was slowly developing from the dialect of the east midlands, as it was spoken in London, not however without contributions from the other dialects (thus the sound *y* in o. eng. gave *i* in London speech, *e* in Kentish, *u* in the west midlands; the words *hill*, *merry* and *shut* bear witness to these variations). The triumph of London speech has often been attributed to Chaucer (*c*. 1340–1400), who was probably a native of London, and there are some grounds for this belief. In his *Canterbury Tales*, mostly written after 1387 under the influence of Boccaccio, Chaucer shows a real linguistic sense. The subtle fun he makes of the French spoken by the Prioress is well known:

> And Frensh she spak ful faire and fetishly,
> After the scole of Stratford atte Bowe,
> For Frensh of Paris was to hir unknowe.

Above all, Chaucer fully grasped the 'gret diversite in English', and deliberately (and probably for the first time) used dialect in literature, making the students in the Reeve's tale speak with a northern one. As was customary at the time, he used the language of London (with features of the dialect of the south, such as *hem* for *them*, *yive* for *give*); it gained popularity from the resounding success of his work, and he was soon to be praised as 'the first finder of our language'. In fact, Chaucer's influence merely hastened or confirmed an evolution which the backing of the most considerable region in fourteenth-century England made practically inevitable: was it not the most densely populated part of the kingdom, containing the capital, the Royal Chancellery, the seat of government and the great universities? The invention of printing finally confirmed the victory of 'standard English'.

Though her history was very different, we see an almost equally decisive victory for French in France. What became of the two domains of *oïl* and *oc*, whose co-existence within a relatively unified kingdom has already been described? In the country of *oïl*, Francian was becoming predominant by the end of the thirteenth century; it was merely a question of establishing itself: Francian was normally used in the Royal Chancellery, whose activities were becoming considerable. Froissart was the last writer in the dialect of Picardy (his final allegiance to the king was also expressed in his own tongue), and all the notable writers of the fifteenth century, including Burgundians, wrote in Francian.

The country of the *langue d'oc* presented a quite different picture, all the more apparent because of the quantity of works written in the vulgar tongue: works of every description, local chronicles, documents concerning practical affairs. But no single work of obvious value stood out from the mass. And literature did not have enough prestige to impose a common norm. The Jeux Floraux represented a touching, rather than an effective experiment: seven bourgeois of Toulouse called upon poets who were prepared to read their poems on 3 May 1324, in the orchard of the Augustines at Toulouse, and rewarded the best with a golden violet, thus founding the *Consistori del Gai Saber*. The *Leys d'Amors*, written in 1356, was an attempt to restore the rules of orthography, phonetics, grammar and prosody. But the results were mediocre. And works in Occitan had a marked dialectal flavour.

So the balance between the two domains of France found its own level. Normally, the king's decrees were written in Latin for the Midi; there were in fact more and more exceptions to this rule during the fifteenth century, but the French of such royal decrees did not go beyond 'the threshold of offices and chancelleries'. The king also sent French-speaking men from the north into the Midi, but they were not always understood by those around them. In 1450 there was still a good deal of ignorance of French; it was for this reason that one of the Comte d'Armagnac's councillors was obliged to negotiate with the English in Latin. Fifty years later, the situation was in flux. It was not only that the royal administration was infiltrating everywhere: a parliament had been sitting at Toulouse since 1444, and its minutes were kept in French. But as early as 1442 the Estates of Languedoc addressed the king in French. Written in Occitan until 1426, the local chronicle of Montpellier, *Le Petit Thalamus*, was resumed after a long break in 1495, and this time in French. By about 1500, there was no doubt that educated circles in the Midi were bilingual: a sign of the prestige of monarchy and French literature alike. In 1539 the king promulgated without opposition the famous decree of Villers-Cotterets, insisting that judgments, inquests and contracts should be expressed 'in the French mother tongue and not otherwise'; it was aimed particularly at Latin, but Occitan was equally affected. Meanwhile the invention of printing had widened the breach.

The linguistic map of the Iberian peninsula was also being simplified, but incompletely and with many doubtful areas. Castilian had definitely established its supremacy as the language of literature. It even invaded the lyrical poetry that had hitherto seemed to be the preserve of Galician and Portuguese: produced at the end of the fourteenth century, the *Cancionero de Baena* was a collection of poems, the earliest of which were still in Galician, but the majority in Castilian; in Portugal itself in the fifteenth century some Portuguese authors wrote their contributions to the *Cancionero de Resende* in Castilian. The dialect of León was even more obviously in retreat than Galician: by the fifteenth century it only existed in the form of a rustic patois, and the classical drama deliberately made peasants speak it as a symbol of their class. Aragonese put up a more stubborn resistance: Juan Fernández de Heredia (*c.* 1310–96) still wrote in Aragonese influenced by Catalan; his successors in the fifteenth century endeavoured to write in the purest possible Castilian.

This was because the political situation had changed. In

1412 the dynasty of Barcelona on the throne of Aragon came to an end, and a branch of the royal family of Castile, the Trastamare, succeeded by means of the Compromis de Caspe. Aragonese, at least as a literary language, could not resist this change of sovereign. The position of Catalan was stronger: Catalan literature of the fourteenth century had been brilliant, and the expression 'the Catalan language' was used increasingly often, showing a high degree of linguistic awareness. The second Castilian king of Aragon, Alfonso the Magnanimous, seems however to have attempted a 'linguistic expansion': when he opened the Barcelona Corts (17 September 1416) he made his 'proposal' in Castilian – which earned him an invitation to love his new country if he wished to be loved by it. He did not insist, and read his 'proposal' in Catalan at the following Corts (1419).

The sovereign in fact depended on financial aid from the Catalans, and the eclipse of the Castilian monarchy weakened his position even more. Things changed when the marriage of Ferdinand and Isabella (1469) brought about the union of Aragon and Castile, when the Catalan rebellion had been crushed (1472), and when the capture of Granada (1492) had set the seal on the triumph of the new monarchy. The years before and after 1500 were marked by more than one sign that Castilian had penetrated the literature of the Catalan countries: the *Jardinet d'Orats* (1486), a collection of Barcelonese lyrics, contained twenty poems in Castilian out of eighty-four; the Roussillon poet Pedro Moner wrote most of his work in Castilian; at Valencia in 1510, the translator Narciso Viñoles prided himself on choosing '*esta limpia, elegante y graciosa lengua castillana . . . entre muchas bárbares y salvajes*' (this pure, elegant and gracious Castilian language . . . among many barbarous and wild ones of Spain). A development pregnant with affronts and difficulties!

Portugal affirmed its independence more felicitously, in spite of marriages and conflicts. The kingdom had absorbed the Algarve in the south, but its new equilibrium was effected by the predominance of the central dialect, that of Lisbon.

Let us turn now to countries whose political and linguistic unification was less advanced. It has often been said of Italy that it was at this period (and for long afterwards) only a geographical expression. Its dissensions and weaknesses, as much as its brilliance and wealth, led to foreign intervention: thus French influence was felt at Genoa and Naples, and Catalan in Sardinia and Sicily; in 1442, the victories of a Castilian sovereign, Alfonso the Magnanimous, set him on the throne of Naples. Nevertheless there was a reaction against these interventions, particularly that of the French: how could Italians, asked Benvenuto d'Imola, learn and admire French, which was in fact no more than the 'bastard daughter of the Latin language'? And when Petrarch was invited to France in 1361 he excused himself on the grounds of his poor knowledge of French.

All the same, there were other factors that favoured a certain degree of linguistic unification. The founding of the great city states – such as Genoa, Milan, Venice and Florence – simplified the political map. Relations between these states were increasing, and politicians went from one to another. The development of trade, the forming of great companies, with a large correspondence circulating between their head office and branches, also had their effect. Colonies of Italian merchants abroad saw the gap between dialects narrowing: in the fifteenth century the *Libro mastro* of the Borromei bank in London provided countless signs of this tendency to Italianism. Another setting favourable to rapprochement was that of students, who came from all over Italy and studied together at Bologna or one of the new universities of Perugia, Florence or Siena. Fully developed public life, important traffic and trade, a high standard of education – Italy held all the trumps except political unity.

In such favourable circumstances, a '*volgare illustre*' owing much to the Tuscan dialect, naturally gained prestige. Dante's influence was prolonged by that of Petrarch, son of a banished Florentine, whose lyric poetry displayed his skill in choosing forms and vocabulary; and by Boccaccio, who wrote his *Decameron* in the Florentine dialect, with noticeable regard for conformity. Dante, Petrarch and Boccaccio: these were the 'three Crowns' of literature. Public readings and innumerable copies bore witness to the pride all cultivated Italians felt in them. 'No other Italian language is more beautiful, nor more proper to be spoken than Florentine', Benvenuto d'Imola concluded.

Petrarch died in 1374, Boccaccio in 1375, and there was no one to replace them. But the humanist reaction was still confined to small groups; no other city could dispute the palm with Florence – Venice and Milan were in the grip of practical affairs, and Rome was crushed by the absence of the popes at Avignon, and the Great Schism; Sicily was too isolated. The Florentine dialect gained ground throughout Italy during the fifteenth century. At Bergamo, at the beginning of the century, Stefano Tiraboschi copied an ancient Veronese poem about Saint Catherine; a comparison of the two texts gives some idea of the extent to which dialectal peculiarities were in retreat:

> *L'imperaor Maxanço clama gi credenderi,*
> *gi baron de la corto et altri cavaleri . . .*

and, in more conformist form:

> *Lo imperadore Masenzo sì giamà li soi credenderi,*
> *li barone de la corte e li altri cavaleri . . .*

In the south, the first version of Iacopo Sannazaro's *Arcadia*, written in about 1490, still had a strong Neapolitan flavour; ten years later, the author, wishing to be understood throughout Italy, rewrote it according to Tuscan rules.

But the success of Florentine was founded above all on its literature. In their daily life at the end of the fifteenth century, Italians spoke their dialects. Tuscan was still the 'Tuscan language', and only in opposition to the speech of foreigners was an Italian language mentioned: '*non sapeva parlare italiano*', was written about an Albanian sailor. This co-existence of vigorous dialects and an almost universal literary language was to characterise Italy for centuries.

Germany in about 1300 – when the Minnesingers' charms had faded, and the power of the Hohenstaufens had crumbled – was the country of five or six very lively *Schrift-dialekte*, and it was not obvious which of them was to carry the day. However, in the course of the next two centuries the situation became clear.

A first noteworthy event was that German became the language of the chancelleries, at the expense of Latin. After the nobility, the towns rallied to it between 1360 and 1380. The German of the chancelleries was evidently quite without literary pretensions; cluttered with clichés, stubbornly respectful of tradition, limited in its lexical horizon, it could nonetheless act as an example and impose the observance of certain rules. Among these chancelleries, the emperor's attracted most notice, and never more than under Charles IV of Luxembourg (1346–78) – an enlightened sovereign who protected writers, was in communication with Petrarch, and who founded the University of Prague. His chancellor, Johann von Neumarkt, was a very cultured man who recruited his staff principally in the west, between the river Main and Trier. Without eclipsing the other chancelleries, that of Charles IV became so famous that it was much imitated. It thus helped fix certain linguistic forms and usages, such as that of *werden* for the future. Its scribes were however of various origins; the deeds drawn up by them show hesitation over important points, such as the sign of the umlaut, or diphthongisation (the proportions of *ei* to *î*, and *au* to *ū*, were about three to two). Moreover, the brilliance of the empire was short-lived, barely surviving Charles IV. And does it not seem paradoxical that the unification of the German language began in Bohemia, a country where the majority of the population spoke Slav?

As they advanced eastwards, the Germans had not always left this basic population of Slavs to live in peace! Massacres and expulsions had often rid medieval Europe of these 'Indians', freeing the land for the colonists who replaced them. A 'Germanic colonial language' was formed, the more comprehensive as these colonists were recruited from various sources: in this connection the frontier region of Meissen deserves special mention. Situated on the route Leipzig–Meissen–Dresden, its central position enabled it to attract Rhenish, Hessians, Bavarians and even people from Flanders and the Alps. The language spoken in this country has been described as '*geistige Mitte zwischen Lübeck und Nürnberg*'. Some idea of it is given us by the chancellery of the Wetteins, which spread the linguistic usages established in the imperial offices at Prague.

At the end of the fifteenth century, however, although the language of Meissen seemed to be vanquishing other High or Middle German dialects – at least in its written form – the Low German dialects had hardly been affected. Then came Luther:

Ich habe keine gewisse, sonderliche, eigne Sprache im deutschen, sondern brauche der gemeinen deutschen Sprache, das mich beide, Ober- und Niderlander, verstehen mögen. Ich rede nach der sechsischen Cantzelei, welcher nachfolgen alle Fürsten und Könige in Deutschland.

(I have no special language of my own in German; I use the common German language, so that both High and Low

Germans may understand me equally well. In speech I follow the Saxon Chancellery; which is imitated by all the princes and kings in Germany.)

In this passage Luther has himself described the effect he had on linguistics. He was not a linguist, language was to him merely the Evangelist's 'scabbard'. His idea of a 'common language' was vague. Yet his position favoured his influence. As a child he had contacts with Low German; as a young man he had studied at Wittenberg, where he spoke the dialect of Meissen. His attachment to this depended on its increasing his audience, and the extraordinary success of his works spread the language he wrote in. This was in fact the Meissen dialect, but with its vocabulary greatly enriched by borrowings from other dialects. Luther was not the father of the German language, as is sometimes said, but he was one of those who most effectively helped construct it, during a long evolution that had still a long way to go.

Imperfectly and unequally, Europe was thus in about 1500 moving towards a general agreement between nation and language. National languages were taking precedence over the dialectal forms; they triumphed over groups of dialects (like Occitan and Low German) now being gradually reduced to a position of inferiority, and over languages considered as foreign (such as French in England and Italy). These developments were accompanied by a rise in linguistic nationalism, whose manifestations became more aggressive in some regions that have kept their enthusiasm to the present day (the Netherlands, Catalonia). During the first centuries of the Middle Ages there had been a natural mistrust of anyone speaking a foreign language, but not nationalism of this sort. From now on, love for the linguistic heritage was to be explicit, both as something noble and beautiful in itself and as the expression of a national entity.

Standardisation of language

The external simplification of the different languages just described was accompanied by internal standardisation. As they gradually became national languages, their old physiognomy disappeared and they became more ordered. This was the period of 'middle' languages everywhere: Middle French, *Mittelhochdeutsch*. It has even been suggested that the written language of England during the fifteenth century should be called 'early modern English'. These changes took effect chaotically, by means of trial and error, and no language yet profited from being spread abroad as it was by printing later on, nor from the rules imposed by grammarians. However, the way was being paved for both these influences. And in due course, modern languages appeared.

1 Orthographical uncertainty was very common in all languages. In Italian, hesitation over velar gutturals and palatals continued, for instance between *cane* and *chane*, *figlio* and *figlo*; the influence of humanism tended towards etymological spellings, which reflected the Latin origins of words. In Spanish, although *h* was slowly gaining ground at the expense of initial *f*, this evolution was not completed until the seventeenth century; but by the fourteenth century the final *-e* was re-established in every case where it was to persist; in the fifteenth century *edad* and *merced* were accepted, and hardly anyone went on writing *edat*, *mercet*, as they had before. In French, there was still indecision between traditional spellings that had kept little touch with developments in pronunciation; orthography by analogy, manifested in a prodigious appearance of *z*'s and *x*'s in terminations; and etymological orthography, rather clumsily attempting to refer to the origins of words, whence *oultre*, *dessoubz*. Scribes who wanted to earn more money by making texts longer cumbered words with useless letters. In

English, terminations in -y increased; in the fourteenth century the letter đ disappeared, and þ also began to give way to the group *th*, although it sometimes persisted in the form of *y* (whence modern archaisms such as: ye olde inn). In Germany, such rules as the suppression of double consonants and the use of a capital for the first letter of a substantive were not accepted until the sixteenth century.

All these languages were spoken long before they were written, and there was never a complete correspondence between pronunciation and orthography. Adjustments were made later, according to different criteria and with greater difficulty when phonetic evolution had been important and complicated. The reign of orthography had not yet begun.

2 Where the sound of words was concerned, a number of problems occurred nearly everywhere. In Italy and Spain, there was a popular reaction against Latinisms: in the former this produced (as against *au*) *altore*, *lalda*; in the latter, *esento* and *perfeto* had moved away from their Latin models. The fate of diphthongs was decided differently in France and Germany. In France, where they had been so numerous in old French, they were now reduced: for instance Villon, by rhyming *royne* with *souveraine* provides us with evidence that *oi* was becoming *ai* in popular speech. In Germany diphthongisation of long vowels became general (*î*, *ū* into *ei*, *au*), especially in accented syllables. The final -*e* effectively became mute in France during the fourteenth century, while still pronounced in England. The physiognomy of languages everywhere was being modernised, much more definitely than was happening in the changing sphere of orthography.

3 In morphology, it is interesting to follow the fate of nominal inflexion: it did not really persist except in Germany whose system of declensions was becoming simpler; but 'by the fifteenth century all casual inflexions had disappeared from

French';[10] in general the objective case triumphed, and certain modern doublets (*sire-seigneur, on-homme*) are all that remain to remind us of the old system of two cases. Plural terminations were standardised everywhere; in Italy certain series were established (in -*i*, in -*ce*); in England, the termination -*es*, which had triumphed in the north, gradually eliminated the southern -*en* (although *children* and *oxen* remained).

The system of inflexion of verbs also became noticeably simpler everywhere. In Italian, the termination -*iamo* became general for the first person plural of the present tense. In Spanish, imperfects and conditionals of the type *sabiés, tenié*, still frequent in the fourteenth century, were afterwards supplanted by *entendias, tenia*. In French, in the present indicative, the form in -*e* was established for the first person singular (*aime*, not *aim*), and the form in -*ons* for the plural. In English the verbal prefix *ge*- was still found in a reduced form (*ybound*) in Chaucer's past participle, but disappeared in the fifteenth century; it persisted in German, but here also conjugations became simpler.

The use of the article had become general in the course of the preceding period between the eleventh to the thirteenth century. Its form was only fixed by degrees. Italian went on hesitating between *il* and *el*; Castilian made a quicker decision, though archaisms like *ell espada* could still be found in the middle of the fifteenth century; in French, the contractions (*ou, dou*) gradually took their modern forms (*au, du*).

4 Syntax everywhere was becoming standardised in the modern manner, even if its evolution was slowed up by the influence of Latin or the weight of tradition. For instance, in French, the disappearance of nominal inflexion did not still involve a full use of form-words: Charles d'Orléans wrote '*es mains dame jeunesse*' (*dans les mains de dame jeunesse*). The

habitual use of the subjective pronoun no longer offset the simplification of verbal forms. The order of words destined to become general in modern French was occurring more frequently: subject – verb – object.

The generalisation of the article was an important feature of the previous period. Its use still had to be standardised in a number of special cases: Italian suppressed the article in the complement of material (Boccaccio wrote '*le colonne del porfido*', but in the fifteenth century the normal construction was '*la palla d'oro*'); Spanish combined the article with a possessive adjective (*la tu torre*) much less frequently than before.

5 The vocabularies of all languages were enormously enriched. This was the natural result of developments in techniques and the arts, and in mentalities. In France, transformed military techniques necessitated a new vocabulary and led to a great many Germanic terms being abandoned. In Italy, a terminology of the fine arts was created (that of architecture owed much to Alberti), and this passed into other languages. The same happened for politics and diplomacy. According to Brunot, about a seventh of the lexical treasure of France is made up of words invented in the fourteenth and fifteenth centuries.

In Italy, Spain and France, a massive invasion of Latinisms took place. Many of these words merely passed through the language and disappeared. Others took root, after provoking strenuous opposition. Some supplanted previous words: in Italy, *esercito*, *orazione*, *republica* replaced *oste*, *diceria* and *comune* in the fourteenth century.

No vulgar tongue had more prestige than that which existed in France in the thirteenth century. It has of course been pointed out that English incorporated a great many French words at this time, but this could only happen as and when the conquerors' language was no longer regarded as an obstacle. In Italy, Petrarch subjected the language to severe scrutiny, and a number of Gallicisms disappeared; on the other hand some Italianisms entered French (*arquebuse*, *banquet*, *canon*, *citadelle*), and also Spanish (*ambuscada*, *belleza*, *lonja*).

Interest in words was general. In his *Morgante*, Pulci noted down technical, rare or even exotic terms, and some were introduced into the language by him – such as *gelosia* for a window with a grille. Slang was studied: a clerk from Dijon made a dictionary of it (1455–8), while the German *Rotwelsch* was preserved for us by several works on the speech of criminals. The vulgar tongue borrowed from dialects everywhere: in the fourteenth century, literary Italian absorbed Venetian *madrigal*, and Paduan *cavezza*; many Occitan words, such as *abeille*, *bourgade*, *cabane*, *cigale*, *escargot* and *salade* were absorbed into French.

Finally, semantic changes must be noted. Some are well known: for instance, in Italy the rediscovery of the values of antiquity diverted words like *virtù*, *piacere* from their Christian meanings. But on the whole 'the internal life of the vocabulary of the period,' says Brunot regretfully, has not been sufficiently studied. There is no doubt that a systematic examination would yield a rich supply of information bearing on mental evolution.

It has of course been impossible in these few lines to present anything approaching a complete picture of the evolution of languages; we have rather attempted to suggest that there was an appreciable advance towards the modern forms, although it was not yet regular or organised. For this the invention of printing and the work of grammarians were needed.

Power of the printing-press

In about 1450 the first printed book was issued by a press, thanks to the discovery of moveable type, still connected with the name of Gutenberg. The new activity spread from Germany throughout the countries of Europe. In 1470 a press was working in Paris, in one of the buildings of the Sorbonne. At the same time books were beginning to be printed in Italy. In 1471–2 an English businessman called Caxton learned the technique from the printers of Cologne; he founded a press at Bruges in 1474 or 1475, with the calligrapher Colard Mansion, and in 1476 he began printing at Westminster. Caxton worked mainly for pleasure, he was a typical bibliophile. But these first printers were men of very different sorts: financiers like Johann Fust (c. 1400–66) who supported Gutenberg; craftsmen of book-production like Peter Schöffer of Mainz (c. 1425–1502) and Nicolas Jenson of Venice (d. 1480), or humanists such as Aldus Manutius of Venice (1450–1515) and Henri Estienne of Paris (c. 1460–1520). Their output was considerable, amounting to more than 35,000 incunabula, or works printed before 1500.

Whatever their origin, printers shared the desire to sell as many copies as possible. So that they should be accessible to the greatest number of readers, it was necessary to eliminate variants of spelling, forms and words, which by their peculiarity might hinder comprehension of the text. This work devolved on correctors, whose influence was pre-eminent in standardising norms. It has been maintained that the correctors of the 100,000 copies of the Bible in German published at Wittenberg had more influence than Luther himself! For they did not feel in the least degree obliged to respect an author's wishes, rather was it incumbent on him to observe their rules if he did not want to be corrected.

The work of the correctors was not always enlightened or unanimous. In France, they accepted the oddities and contradictions of manuscripts, leaving practically the whole task of clarification to the grammarians. In Germany, several 'schools' were in opposition for some time – Rhenish, Alemannic, Bavarian, Nurembergian, Saxon – until, during the sixteenth century, agreement was enforced according to the norms of the chancelleries. In England, Caxton's activity seems to have been more carefully considered and successful; by printing the works of Chaucer, Gower, Lydgate and Malory he ensured the definite triumph of the dialect of the eastern midlands.

The geographical situation of printing presses seems to have been pregnant with consequences. In Italy, Venice was one of the chief centres, and printers propagated the Venetian dialect, already strongly influenced by Florentine; among many examples we may cite the spellings *a lui, di lui, con lui*, which triumphed over *a llui, di lui, co llui*, because Venetians were unaware of assimilations due to syntactic phonetics. In southern France, books printed at Lyons had the widest circulation, and provided French texts for learned men; the rapid spread of the *langue d'oïl* is thus explained. 'It was not Simon de Montfort, but Gutenberg who gallicised Languedoc.'[11]

At all events, the invention of printing did more service to the vulgar tongue than to Latin. Of course many works in Latin were printed; the presses of university towns, like Bologna and Rome in Italy, devoted themselves specially to Latin, for the benefit of students. But a large number of copies of Latin manuscripts had already been made. Before the invention of printing, copies of Latin manuscripts were very much more numerous than any others, and also less expensive. This ratio was reversed by printing. The new conditions of rentability made it possible to print works of literature in the vulgar tongue for a cultured public: in the year 1472 alone, three editions of the *Divine Comedy* were published, at Foligno, Mantua and Venice (or Iesi).

The influence of printing was not fully in operation until the sixteenth century. However, in 1500 the number of readers was already impossible to calculate. They experienced the same intellectual revolution that a child knows when his mind first begins to react to the process of reading words. Literary language gained new power. Printing crowned the work of standardisation, clarification and normalisation that was going on, not without hesitation and confusion, as a result of linguistic evolution in general. It was now the grammarians' turn to give judgment.

Stammerings of linguistic theory

No true linguistic science existed in medieval times. There was a lack of material on which it could be based: Latin was the only scientific means of expression worthy of study. Moreover, linguistic events seemed to lack that universal and abstract character that was considered an indispensable foundation for a science – that is to say, knowledge that was general and certain.

Yet the structure of language was the object of much thought. It was necessary to establish principles by which the writings of the Fathers of the Church could be understood. An exact terminology must be decided on, recognised by all, for discussing scholastic problems. Thought must be given to the relations between the various aspects of a word as a symbol: it was a sound (*vox*) produced by a physiological process depending on natural science; it denoted a special reality (*dictio*), and the union of *vox* and *dictio* was one of the objects of psychology; finally it belonged to a grammatical category (*pars orationis*, *modus significandi*). 'Speculative grammar', taught by the Faculty of Arts, was specially devoted to this last aspect. It was the logic of language, as universal as the rules of reason. Belief in its importance inspired clumsy efforts to copy the grammars of the vulgar tongues from that of Latin.

This activity of the *modistae* (or those who studied the *modus significandi*) was connected with the whole body of medieval thought, and made an indispensable contribution to it. On a much humbler level, the necessities of practical life were also forcing linguistic thought to hazard its first steps. Several treatises were written for the use of travellers in distant lands, especially pilgrims and missionaries. In the eleventh and twelfth centuries, guides offered visitors to the Holy Places little vocabularies of Greek, and later Arabic and even Hebrew (in one established case); the pilgrims' guide to Compostela set out some fifteen Basque words, particularly useful when crossing that uncivilised country. As time passed, this form of literature developed. In the library of Charles v, King of France, there was a work on 'pilgrimages across the sea and how to obtain the necessaries of life in the Saracen tongue'. At the end of the fifteenth century a nobleman from Cologne, Arnold von Harff, visited the Holy Places and the chief sanctuaries of Europe; an indefatigable traveller, he went from Ethiopia and Turkey to Spain and France, making as he went nine little practical vocabularies of essential words and phrases – in Albanian, Arabic, Basque, Breton, Croat, Greek, Hebrew, Hungarian and Turkish.

In the thirteenth century, missionary activity in African and Asiatic countries was carried on by mendicant friars. The illusion that their converts would finally learn to speak Latin did not fade; Pope John xxII suggested that the king of Armenia should make his subjects learn it; in 1338, a mission leaving for Peking carried Latin grammars in its baggage; the Catalan Ramon Llull, who did so much to promote the study of foreign languages, believed that Latin was destined to become a universal language and means of understanding between all men. Meanwhile it was necessary to study the language of the races to be converted, and provide them with any available translations of sacred texts. In 1311, the Council of Vienna foresaw that in each of the universities of Paris, Oxford, Bologna and Salamanca, as well as in the Curia, two chairs of Hebrew, two of Greek, two of Arabic and two of Chaldean would be instituted – an over-ambitious programme, there being an insufficiency of teaching staff. This intellectual movement left traces, however: for instance, in about 1303 a compilation was made of a Latin-Persian-Couman vocabulary, a Couman grammar and several religious texts in that language. This was used during the conversion of the Coumans in what is today Romania. The Couman language having disappeared in the eighteenth century, this *Codex Cumanicus* remains irreplaceable evidence for us today.

A very different sort of undertaking consisted in making a literary language more easy to understand with a view to enlarging its international audience. In the thirteenth century the success of lyrical poetry in Occitan inspired the production of grammars of that language: such were the *Razos de trobar* of the Catalan Ramon Vidal de Besalù, and the *Donatz proensals*, compiled by Huc Faidit for two Italian noblemen.

The co-existence in one country of populations expressing themselves in different languages posed problems which had to be solved. In Spain under Moorish rule bilingual texts of the Bible were made, and a Latin-Arabic dictionary, now at Leiden, bears witness to a scholarly study of Arabic in the twelfth century, and is remarkably free from religious polemics. Such endeavours continued and may be said to have culminated in the grammar of the Moorish dialect of Granada, composed in about 1500 by the Hieronymite monk Pedro de Alcalá.

In the Low Countries, French came face to face with Germanic dialects. And ever since the end of the thirteenth century Bruges had been a great international centre of trade and banking: so that it is not surprising that dictionaries and conversation manuals were compiled there.

The trilingualism of at least the more cultivated circles in England has been emphasised. As French began to be thought of as a foreign language, lexical and grammatical literature was enriched, the most striking examples being the *Volume of Vocabularies* composed by Walter de Bibelsworth for a noble lady (*c.* 1300), the *Orthographia gallica*, an attempt to correct the faults made by the islanders (first half of the fourteenth century), John Barton's *Donait françois* (*c.* 1400) and, lastly, Caxton's *Dialogues in French and English* (1483).

The study of the ancient languages led to similar undertakings. For a long time students had used grammars entirely
written in Latin, but during the thirteenth century grammars
based on the vulgar tongue of those concerned began to
appear. An example is a little Latin-Italian grammar, perhaps
compiled in the region of Verona (or so it would appear from
the many Italian words and turns of phrase quoted), now
preserved at Munich. Methods of learning Latin improved
with the success of the humanist movement. Greek was again
studied, after being so completely neglected for centuries that
very strange distortions remained unnoticed in the lists of
words (for instance, the maxim *Gnôthi seauton*, know yourself,
had become *Gnotosolitos*, from which it was deduced that the
word *litos* could mean 'oneself' as well as 'stone'!) An ap-
prenticeship to Hebrew was even thought desirable for those
studying the Scriptures, and contacts between Jews and Christians had prevented it being completely lost.

Some knowledge of linguistics was acquired through translations, which had steadily broadened their scope ever since the
Carolingian epoch – until it might be fair to say that the
translator and the copyist were the Atlantes of medieval
culture. Unfortunately no general study has been made of the
art of translation as practised during these centuries. The
absence of systematic rules, and the mediocre quality of many
of the productions is certainly to be deplored. As a whole the
tradition was one of literal translation. It must be remembered
that the translator did not move from one fully evolved
language to another; he usually found himself faced with two
different levels of linguistic development: on one hand Latin,
with its grammatical rules and lexical traditions; on the other a
vulgar tongue, incomplete as to vocabulary and lacking any
elaborate grammatical structure. One may well suppose that
literal translations would help supplement these deficiencies in
young languages.

In the course of this study, we have commented on various

grammars composed to supply practical needs. But their too strict dependence on Latin grammar, strengthened by a belief in the universal value of speculative grammar, interfered with their efficiency. However, in the fifteenth century there were signs of a movement to break free from Donat and Priscian. Alberti may have been the author of the *Regole della lingua fiorentina*, which belonged to the Medici Library in 1495, and of which we possess a copy dated 1508: it makes an appreciable attempt to fix the norms for the Florentine dialect, without encumbering itself with declensions and long-vanished grammatical data. In August 1492, soon after the fall of Granada, when Christopher Columbus was on his way to America, a *Gramática* by Antonio de Nebrija was printed in Spain, which represents the most complete attempt of this sort for the period. Nebrija clearly conceived the project of giving Castilian its own grammatical norms, respecting its originality and assuring it a permanence comparable to that of Latin and Greek, in order, as he wrote:

> *Lo que agora i de aqui adelante en él se escriviere, pueda quedar en un tenor i estenderse por toda la duración de los tiempos que están por venir, como vemos que se ha hecho en la lengua griega y latina, has cuales, aunque sobre ellas han passado muchos siglos, todaviá quedan en una uniformidad.*

(What now and henceforward is written in it shall remain in the same tenor and so continue for all time, as we see has happened in the Greek and Latin languages, which, although many centuries have passed over them, still maintain their uniformity.)

Nebrija was writing to ensure the triumph of the Castilian language and its acceptance by all the new subjects of the Catholic sovereigns. His work shows linguistic nationalism in the ascendant, as well as the ability of languages to become, little by little, completely standardised. It is hard to conceive how this could have happened without printing, which enabled them to be understood by all. Of course we cannot fail to be struck by Nebrija's naïve belief in the permanence of language, and by his lack of that historical sense of which signs were already appearing in the fifteenth century. Were they not discussing at Florence, for instance, in 1435, in the antichamber of Pope Eugenius IV, the possibility that there was a similar difference between literary Latin and the spoken language in ancient Rome, to that separating fifteenth-century Latin from the vulgar tongues? The grammarians' reign was beginning; they would act normatively, and set themselves to standardise correct usage. That is an important event for historians. The days of free linguistic development were over. There would no longer be a 'vulgar tongue'.

Chapter Seven
CONCLUSION

WE HAVE TRIED to give a brief description of a phenomenon which relates at the same time to comparative linguistics, social history and the collective psychology of language.

From the linguistic point of view, it was a movement of divergence from Latin and Germanic, and of convergence to the advantage of the modern languages of western Europe. But, strictly speaking, both movements were present in the whole evolutionary process. Moreover, the Romance and Germanic languages carried out fruitful exchanges which were favoured in their turn by the Roman conquest, the establishment of Germanic populations in *Romania*, and later on the conquest of England by the Normans. One might say that French is the most Germanic of the Romance languages, and English the most Romance of the Germanic languages. In fact each language possesses it own special physiognomy and traces its own graph. Yet all have characteristics in common.

This is because they all evolved in a similar social setting, which produced clearly defined tendencies in them. We must first emphasise the important influence of Christianity on linguistic evolution. It introduced into the heart of the Roman world, and then among the Germanic races, a whole collection of feelings, ideas, dogmas, institutions and rituals, all entirely new and expressed in more or less inter-related words and formulas. It provided a common linguistic basis between these divergent Romance languages themselves, as well as between them and the developing Germanic languages (and others also). Unity of faith was expressed in linguistic terms. Christianity also led many people to speak or write in order to expound and propagate their faith, although they would not otherwise have ventured to do so. To reveal the truths that seemed to them so sublime they used very simple language. The supremacy of the literary language was thus challenged, until new literary languages appeared. This popular or 'vulgar' origin of language was a phenomenon of the greatest significance.

We must also stress the range of the demographic, economic and social movement that had been in operation at least since the ninth century. The domain of language was extending both quantitatively and qualitatively everywhere. Men were more numerous, and each of them spoke more and on more varied subjects, both because human contacts in country districts were commoner, and because the towns provided new opportunities for exchange and collective life. At the same time the development of production and trade, acquisition of new techniques, further division of labour, growing complexity of social life, flowering of art, literature and thought, engendered a vast semantic expansion, in which historians have taken increasing interest. The phenomenon contained many nuances, but it was present almost everywhere, as is shown by the striking enrichment of the various languages.

Among linguistic changes, there is one that should be stressed. The ancient languages were to a large extent synthetic: they expressed the nature and function of the words by inflective endings (see pages 22–4). Gradually, in the written language – and no doubt sooner in speech – nouns and verbs began to be preceded by form-words, entrusted with the tasks formerly given to the terminations, which simultaneously tended to vanish. These were the article, the personal pronoun and the preposition.

The article has given psychologists and linguists much food for thought. Gustave Guillaume has attempted to explore its significance, though his theory has not received a unanimous vote. The article solved the problem which arose at the very moment when man's mind became aware of the difference between a noun before use – the mere potentiality of naming various things – and a noun used to name one or several things. The word 'man' potentially indicates the species as well as an individual, or intermediate realities. From the sum-total of a noun's potential meanings one must be chosen and extracted. This is precisely the part played by the article: *l'homme*, *un homme*, *des hommes*. Gustave Guillaume emphasises the significance of this acquisition:

> Objectified language is a 'turning-point' in the history of thought and language. It is the culmination of a development: instead of making us think directly of ideas, speech makes us indirectly think of the relation between these ideas, stabilised to some extent, and our much more mobile and fleeting thoughts. When one says in French *l'homme* or *un homme*, what the article extracts from the mind is the relation between the momentary, particular idea and the permanent universal idea deposited as it were in the language. Here is a real revolution in the expressive system.

Even if we do not follow Gustave Guillaume in his further analysis, there is no doubt that the creation of the article was an extremely important event. Unfortunately, there exists no general study of its appearance in the Romance and Germanic languages. We can only establish one or two landmarks here and there. Appearing early in Greek, the article always originated in a demonstrative pronoun: *ille* in the Romance languages, the demonstrative Indo-European stem **so*, **to* in Greek, and later in English and German. It could be directly demonstrative, by indicating a present object, pointing to it as it were ('this table in front of me'). Or in the second degree it could be indirect: by naming something already referred to and present in memory ('the table that I spoke about, that I am thinking of'). This can be described as an anaphoric movement. When these two movements, the purely demonstrative and the anaphoric, were regularly arranged according to definite and different signs, the article was born.

When can we consider this event to have happened? No complete investigation of this question has been undertaken, and the answer would doubtless vary from one language to another. To confine ourselves to French, the earliest texts make extremely little use of what was to become the article: '*Si Lodhuvigs sagrament* (not: *le serment*) *que son fradre Karlo jurat, conservat*', says the Strasbourg Oath (see page 92). However, we find the definite article in the *Chanson de Roland* (end of the eleventh century): '*Li frein sunt d'or, les seles d'argent mises*'. (The bits are of gold and the saddles made of silver). Its use only very gradually became general: by the seventeenth century we may consider that the article had become a common grammatical tool. But by the end of the twelfth century the encyclopedist Alexander Neckam has provided us with a valuable landmark, by comparing the languages that used the article – Hebrew, Greek, English and French – with Latin, which did without it. The normal use of the article must therefore have been consciously grasped at the time.

The appearance of the personal pronoun in French has been thoroughly studied by Gerald Moignet. We see that personal pronouns in modern French are of two different types. Some of them really indicate living beings, whence they have been given the name of ontic pronouns. They can be used after a preposition, like substantives, or after an expression like *c'est* (*après moi, c'est moi*); they are then called predicative. Thus they can fulfil various syntactical functions without change of form. This is the case with *moi, toi, soi, lui* or *elle, nous, vous, eux* or *elles*. They function as nouns.

Other pronouns – and they are more truly pronouns – indicate behaviour, and are connected with verbs from which they cannot be separated: they have been called existential pronouns. They are not predicative. On the contrary they are confined to their own syntactical function: subjective *je* is opposed to objective *me*; subjective *il* to *le*, *la* or *lui*, which are objective in different ways. Except in a few cases (*lui*, *nous*, *vous*) this difference of thought is expressed by the use of different terms.

This system did not exist in Latin, which possessed many pronouns of the first or ontic type. These remained as autonomous as the substantive, even in regard to the verb. But the existential subjective pronoun did not exist, or rather it was expressed by the inflexion of the verb: it was this which indicated whether it was a question of the first person singular (*curro*) or the third (*currit*). At most, there can be observed in post-classical Latin certain phenomena heralding future changes: the subjective pronoun of the first and second persons is more often explicit, and a pronoun for the third person (*ille*) even makes its appearance. Morphological innovations produce the reduced forms: *mi*, *lo* . . .

Old French contributed many innovations in relation to Latin. For one thing, in the objective case, pronouns were divided into two series, one entirely new: these were existential pronouns connected with a verb. The unstressed forms *me*, *te*, constructed from Latin pronouns, were used to indicate them. For another, the personal form of the verb was isolated by analysis: this was less often expressed by inflexion, and more often by a subjective pronoun. In the earliest French texts, this subjective personal pronoun is on average absent four times for each time that it is present. In the first narrative of the *Roman de Renart* (second half of the twelfth century), it was almost as often absent as present. And after the beginning of the thirteenth century the pronoun prevailed, at first in popular texts apparently. It is extremely likely that these developments reflected others in the spoken language. Finally, the system of pronouns was completed by *on*, which gradually emerged from the Latin *homo*, and emptied itself of content to become a thought form, indicating an undefined agent. The first example appeared in *Alexis*, an anonymous poem and one of the first in the *langue d'oïl*: '*Sainz Boneface, que l'um martir apelet*' (l. 566). This development should therefore be placed in the tenth or at the beginning of the eleventh century.

The true ontic pronoun appeared in Middle French between the end of the thirteenth and the end of the fifteenth centuries. On the one hand, the objective pronoun was more and more often made to play the part of subject: in the fourteenth century people no longer said '*je et N*', but '*moi et N*'; '*c'est moi*' took the place of '*ce sui(s) je*' etc. On the other hand the subjective *elle* took over the functions of a predicative pronoun in the objective case. But the use of the subjective personal pronoun became more and more common, and by the seventeenth century it was obligatory. Developments that had begun in Old French were emphasised and confirmed. The modern system of personal pronouns was virtually established.

The development of the article and personal pronoun were two instances of a more general phenomenon, one which consisted in no longer expressing functions by terminations and inflections, but by words preceding the inflected term. It might be called a process of 'de-inflexion': inflexion gradually ceased to play a part and then disappeared altogether, to be replaced by form-words. This was certainly the result of analysis, as was the entrusting to the preposition (*aptus ad aliquam rem*) of the function hitherto solely given to the case-endings of the substantive (*aptus alicui rei*: dative). This last development began in Latin, as we have seen. The result was a mixed system, in which meanings were supplied both by terminations and prepositions. However, the emphasis was more often on the latter, and the former lost value and interest. It is explained that Gregory of Tours failed to grasp the distinction between accusative and ablative (according to whether there was movement or not) after such prepositions as *in* and *sub*, and that this was one of his chief 'faults' (see page 70).

This general development was obviously leading from synthetic to analytic languages. We have made it clear that alongside literary Latin, which was markedly synthetic, there existed a 'vulgar' Latin, which was much less so. But the developments we have described in French affected all languages to some extent. German, for example, went on leaving inflexions an important part to play; its analytic character was not so clear. The chronology of the phenomena and their separate stages (which need not necessarily be the same everywhere) should be established. Will such a study confirm our present impression – namely that the period contained between the tenth century and the end of the thirteenth saw the most important innovations?

And, finally, a last important question arises concerning the origins, the deep-lying causes of these developments, and of linguistic changes in general. Many writers have adopted the traditional phonetic explanation as a rule: the changes are due to weakened word-endings and inflective terminations, and this has been given the status of a fundamental law. The form-words – article, pronoun and preposition – were according to this view invented to supply the lost terminations. This type of argument is increasingly out of favour today. Is it possible to suppose that mere blind phenomena of pronunciation, which were to be permanent into the bargain, should be enough to cause innovations in the sphere of thought, amounting to a unique stage of development? Surely it is rather the opposite that has happened! Was it not because the function given to terminations was transferred by analytic thinking to the form-words it had created, that the terminations lost their value and were more or less condemned to disappear? Let us look again at de Saussure's subtle and suggestive analysis, quoted on page <s>5</s>. 14.

We are therefore led to give first importance to the psychological data themselves. The state of a language reflects the state of thought, which is primordial. It is not a question of denying the rather absurd effects of the laws of phonics and analogy. But thought makes use of such modifications to construct an even more expressive and subtle linguistic system. As Gustave Guillaume says: 'the ordering of phenomena never consists in demanding mentalism for physicism, but always physicism for mentalism'. This is what endows linguistics with significance for the historian: it gives him access to the deepest evolutionary processes of the human mind.

> In the course of its multimillenary history . . . we see the human mind (as language penetrates its development more deeply) forging for itself and perfecting language as an ever more powerful instrument of thought, through whose increasing power man has slowly developed from a primitive to a civilised being.[12]

The period we have been studying, when the Romance and modern Germanic languages were developing, certainly seems to have constituted a decisive stage in this fundamental evolution.

12/8/2003

NOTES

1 Ferdinand de Saussure, *Cours de linguistique générale*, Paris: Payot, 1916, pp. 252–3.

2 Ibid, pp. 210–11.

3 Roch Valin, Introduction to G. Guillaume, *Langage et science du langage*, Paris: Nizet; Fr. University of Laval, Quebec, 1964.

4 Dag Norberg, 'A quelle époque a-t-on cessé de parler Latin en Gaule?' in *Annales E.S.C.*, March–April 1966, pp. 351–2.

5 Mgr. J. Schrijnen, 'Le latin chrétien devenu langue commune', in *Revue des études latines*, 1934, pp. 99–100.

6 M. Bonnet, *Le Latin de Grégoire de Tours*, Paris: Hachette, 1890, p. 522.

7 Marc Bloch, *La société féodale*, I *La formation des liens de dépendance*, Paris: Albin Michel, 1939, pp. 121–6.

8 Chr. Mohrmann, 'Le dualisme de la latinité médiévale', in *Revue des études latines*, 1951, p. 244.

9 Chr. Mohrmann, ibid., p. 347.

10 F. Brunot, *Histoire de la langue française* . . . , vol. 1, Paris: Colin, 1905, p. 432 of the 1966 edition.

11 E. Le Roy Ladurie, p. 313, *Histoire du Languedoc* ed. Ph. Wolff. Toulouse: Privat, 1967.

12 Roch Valin, *see* note 3.

BIBLIOGRAPHY

1 Introduction

General works The bibliography on the subject is enormous. It is impossible to do more than indicate here a few works which were of particular use to the author, or which carry certain of his conclusions further. Although published some while ago (1916), Ferdinand de Saussure's *Cours de linguistique générale* (Paris: Payot) is still worth consulting. A translation by Wade Baskin, *Course in General Linguistics*, was published in 1960 by Peter Owen, London. This can be supplemented by such up-to-date works as André Martinet's *Eléments de linguistique générale* (Paris: Colin, 1961) which has since been published in a translation by Elizabeth Palmer as *Elements of General Linguistics* (Chicago: Chicago University Press; London: Faber, 1964). A very important book is Walter von Wartburg's *Einführung in Problematik und Methodik der Sprachwissenschaft* (Tubingen: Neimeyer, 1943). See also: Leonard Bloomfield, *Language* (New York: Holt; London: Allen & Unwin, 1935); Mario Pei, *The World's Chief Languages* (New York: Vanni; London: Allen & Unwin, 1949); C. F. Hockett, *A Course in Modern Linguistics* (New York: Macmillan, 1958); H. A. Gleason, *An Introduction to Descriptive Linguistics*, (revised edn., New York: Holt, 1966).

Separate languages For the Romance languages in general see first of all the excellent book by the late W. D. Elcock, *The Romance Languages* (London: Faber; New York: Macmillan, 1960). Then follow up with: Ferdinand Brunot, *Histoire de la langue française, des origines à nos jours*, vol. I (Paris: Colin, 1905; reprinted 1966); Pierre Bec, *La Langue occitane* (Paris: P.U.F., 1963); Rafael Lapesa, *Historia de la lengua española*

(Madrid: Escelicer, 2nd edn., 1950); S. Silva Neto, *Historia de la lingua portuguesa* (Rio de Janeiro: Livros de Portugal, 1962); Bruno Migliorini, *Storia della lingua italiana* (Florence: Sanzone, 2nd edn., 1960). This last has been published in a revised version, recast by T. Gwynfor Griffiths, as *The Italian Language* (London: Faber; New York: Barnes & Noble, 1966). For the Germanic languages see: Hans Eggers, *Deutsche Sprachgeschichte: I Das Althochdeutsche, II Das Mittelhochdeutsche* (Rowohlt, 1963–5); Ernest Tonnelat, *Histoire de la langue allemande* (Paris, 5th edn., 1952), also translated by D. P. Inskip as *History of the German Language* (London: Harrap, 1937); Fernand Mossé, *Esquisse d'une histoire de la langue anglaise* (Lyons: I.A.C., 1958).

2 Remote origins

K. Baldinger, *Die Herausbildung der Sprachräume auf der Pyrenäenhalbinsel* (Berlin: Akademie Verlag, 1958); G. Dottin, *La Langue gauloise* (Paris: Klincksieck, 1920); F. Falc'hun, *Histoire de la langue Bretonne d'après la géographie linguistique* (Paris: Presses Universitaires de France, 1963); R. Menéndez Pidal, *Toponomia prerománica hispana* (Madrid: Editorial Gredos, 1952); F. Mossé, *Manuel de la langue gotique* (Paris: Aubier, 1956); G. Rohlfs, *Die lexikalische Differenzierung der romanischen Sprachen* (Munich: Beck, 1954); E. Schwarz, *Goten, Nordgermanen, Angelsachen. Studien zur Ausgliederung der germanischen sprachen* (Berne: Francke, 1951).

3 The period of formation

The initial change from Latin E. Auerbach, *Literary language and its public in late Antiquity and the Middle Ages*, trans. R. Manheim (New York: Pantheon; London: Routledge & Kegan Paul, 1965); F. Lot, 'A quelle époque a-t-on cessé de parler Latin?' *Archivum Latinitatis Medii Aevi*, 1931; C. Mohrmann, *Etudes sur le Latin des Chrétiens* (also available in English) (Rome: Edizione di Storia e Letteratura, 1958–61); D. Norberg, 'A quelle époque a-t-on cessé de parler Latin en Gaule?', *Annales E.S.C*, 1966; G. Straka, 'La dislocation linguistique de la Romania et la formation des langues romanes à la lumière de la chronologie relative des changements phonétiques', *Revue de linguistique romane*, 1956.

The contribution of the invasions M. Bonnet, *Le Latin de Grégoire de Tours* (Paris: Hachette, 1890); E. Gamillscheg, *Romania Germanica* (Berlin-Leipzig: de Gruyter, 1934–6); M. Gysseling, 'La Genèse de la frontière linguistique dans le Nord de la Gaule', *Revue de Nord*, 1962; Henri Muller, Fr. *L'époque mérovingienne, essai de synthèse de philologie et d'histoire* (New York: Vanni, 1945); G. L. Trager, 'The use of the Latin demonstratives (especially ille and ipse) up to AD 600 as the source of the Roman article' (New York, 1932); J. Vielliard, *Le Latin des diplomes royaux et chartes privées de l'époque mérovingienne* (Paris: Champion, 1927); W. von Wartburg, *Die Ausgliederung der romanischen Sprachraume* (Berne: Francke, 1950).

4 The Tower of Babel

Refer to the extraordinary mine of information in Arno Borst's *Der Turmbau von Babel, Geschichte der Meinungen über Ursprung und Vielfalt der Sprachen und Völker* (Stuttgart, 4 vols., 1957–63).

5 Crystallisation

The free use of histories of the different languages should be completed by: V. H. Galbraith, 'Nationality and Language in Medieval England', *Transactions of the Royal Historical Society*, 1941; R. Menéndez Pidal, *Orígenes del español* (Madrid: Espasa Calpe, 1950); F. Mossé, *Manuel de l'anglais du Moyen Age, II Moyen Anglais* (2nd edn., Paris: Aubier, 1959); *A Handbook of Middle English*, trans. J. A. Walker (Baltimore: Johns Hopkins Press, 1952); H. Paul, *Mittelhochdeutsche Grammatik* (19th edn., editor W. Mitzka, Tubingen: Niemeyer, 1963); Richard Middlewood Wilson, 'English and French in 1100–1300', *History XXVII*, 1943.

6 From Dante to Caxton, Luther and Nebrija

Dante's works have been edited by A. Marigo, see *De vulgari eloquentia ridotto a miglior lezione, comentato e tradotto, Opere di Dante, VI* (Florence: Le Monnier, 3rd edn., 1957). Still very useful is Auguste Brun's *Recherches historiques sur l'introduction du français dans les provinces du Midi* (Paris: Champion, 1923).

There can be no question of giving a bibliography of the origins of printing here. As an introduction, however, see Lucien Febvre and H. J. Martin, *L'Apparition du livre* (Paris: Michel, 1958).

For ideas about linguistics see: Bernard Bischoff, 'The study of Foreign Languages in the Middle Ages' (*Speculum*, XXXVI); G. Bonfante, 'Ideas on the kinship of the European Languages from 1200 to 1800' (*Cahiers d'histoire mondiale*, I); H. Roos, 'Sprachdenken im Mittelalter'

(*Classica et Medievalia*, 1948). Nebrija's grammar has been edited several times. The last edition was by P. Galindo and L. Ortiz (Madrid: Edición de la Junta del Centenario, 1946).

7 Conclusion

For the analysis of psychological changes underlying the linguistic developments described, it will be useful to study the ideas presented in Gustave Guillaume's *Le Problème de l'article et sa solution dans la langue française* (Paris: Hachette, 1919), and his *Langage et science du langage* (Paris: Nizet; Québec: Presses de l'Université Laval, 1948). The historical perspective lacking in these works can be found in Gerard Moignet's *Essai sur le mode subjonctif en latin postclassique et en ancien français* (Paris: Presses Universitaires de France, 2 vols, 1959), and his *Le pronom personnel français, essai de psychosystématique historique* (Paris: Klicksieck, 1965). There are some extremely interesting suggestions for research here.

ACKNOWLEDGMENTS

I should like to say how much I owe to conversations with my colleagues and friends at the University of Toulouse, especially André Nougué, Jean Séguy, Joseph Verguin, and to thank them warmly.

Acknowledgment for the maps is due to the following sources: 69 L. Musset, *Les invasions, les vagues germaniques*, Paris, PUF, 1965; 73 W. D. Elcock, *The Romance Languages*, London, Faber and Faber, 1960; 158, 159, 207, 209 F. Mossé, *Esquisse d'une histoire de la langue anglaise*, Lyon, IAC, 1947; 160 E. Tonnelat, *Histoire de la langue allemande*, Paris, Colin, 1927; 181 R. Lapesa, *Historia de la lengua espanola*, Madrid, 1950; 222–3 L. Febvre and H. J. Martin, *L'apparition du livre*, Paris, 1958. The original maps were drawn by Design Practitioners.

The eight maps that appear in this edition were redrawn by John Gilkes.

INDEX

Abelard, 147
Abrogans Glossary, 94
Aelfric, 99, 102
Alans, 52
Alberti, Leon Battista, 156, 178
Albigensians, 107, 112, 141
Alcalá, Pedro de, 176
Alcuin, 90
Aldus Manutius, 172
Alemanni, 52
Alfonso the Chaste, 115, 134
Alfonso the Learned, 134, 136
Alfonso the Magnanimous, 161, 162
Alfred the Great, 93, 98, 118–19
analytic language, 11–12, 186
Angles, 53, 54, 55, 74
Anglo-Saxon *see* Old English
Anno, Archbishop of Cologne, 125
Annolied, 125
Apollinaris, Sidonius, 43
Arabic, 55, 63–4, 131, 176
Arbeo, Bishop of Freising, 94
Arnobius, 66
articles (definite and indefinite), 68, 169, 182–3
Auerbach, 102–3

Augustine of Hippo, St, 50, 85, 86–7, 88

Babel, Tower of, 82–3
Bacon, Roger, 112
Baldinger, Karl, 45–6
Baltic, 22
barbarian invasions, 52–65
Barton, John, 176
Basque, 34, 35, 54, 132, 137
Benedict of Aniane, 91
Beowulf, 98
Berbers, 63, 64
Bernard de Chartres, 147
Bernard de Clairvaux, 147
Bésalu, Ramon Vidal de, 176
Bibelsworth, Walter de, 176
Bloch, M., 1–2, 103
Boccaccio, 153, 158, 163
Boecis, 99
Boëthius, 88, 97, 99
Book of the Eighth Sphere, 136
Book of the Evangelists, 95
Breton, 22, 33, 54, 55
Brun, A., 32
Brunot, 170, 171
Brut, 121, 122

Brythonic, 22, 33
Burgundians, 52, 61

Cancionero de Baena, 160
Cancionera de Resende, 160
Cantar de mio Cid, 133–4
Canterbury Tales, 158
Canticles of the Virgin, 134
Capetian dynasty, 107, 113
Carolingian period, 89–93, 110;
    renaissance, 90, 94, 103, 108
Cassel Glossary, 94–5
Castilian, 32, 35, 113, 132, 133–4,
    136–8, 155–6, 160, 161, 169,
    178
Catalan, 22, 33, 46, 65, 108, 132,
    133, 134–5, 138–9, 161
Caxton, W., 157, 172, 173, 176
Celtic languages, 22, 33–4, 74
Certamo coronario (1441), 156
Cesarius of Arles, St, 50, 103
Charlemagne, 89–91, 124, 139
Charles the Bald, 92
Charles iv of Luxembourg, 164
Chaucer, Geoffrey, 120, 158
Chilperic, 58
Chrétien de Troyes, 112–13
Christianity, 15, 36, 47–51, 72, 76–7,
    79, 80–89, 91, 141, 146, 180–81
Cicero, 23, 27, 66
Clamanges, Nicolas de, 155
Clovis, 52, 53
Codex Argenteus, 37
Col, Gontier, 155
Conon de Béthune, 113
Consolation of Philosophy, 97
Cornish, 22
Corpus Inscriptionum Latinarum, 25–6
Couman, 175–6
Crónica General, 136

Crusades, 105
Cyprian, St, 66
Cyril, St, 92–3

Danes, 118–20
Dante, 115, 143, 144–6, 149–51,
    152, 153, 155, 163
De Civitate Deo, 85
De vulgari eloquentia, 145, 149–51
De rebus Hispaniae, 151
Decameron, 163
dialects, 18–20
Dialogue of the Exchequer, 121
Dialogues in French and English, 176
Divine Comedy, The, 145, 173
Donait François, 176
Donat, 92, 146, 178
Donatz proensals, 176
Dottin, G., 33
Dutch, 40, 75, 129–30

Eckhart, Meister, 128, 153
Edward i, King of England, 122
Egeria, 50, 51, 66–8
Eggers, H., 2, 77, 124
Einhard, 90, 103
Elcock, W.D., 2
Eneit, 130
English
    in period of formation, 74
    early literature, 79, 98–9, 102,
        115–16
    crystallisation, 104, 115–24
    later developments, 152, 153,
        157–8, 167, 168, 169, 170–71
    other references, 10, 17, 39, 42,
        72, 75, 93, 180, 182
Estienne, Henri, 172
Eulalia, St, 99
Eugenius iv, Pope, 179

Faidit, Huc, 176
Falc'hun, Abbé, 33, 54
Ferdinand of Aragon, 161
Finnish, 38
'first mutation', 38–9
form words, 8, 11, 181–6
Fust, Johann, 172
Francian, 113–14, 159
Francis of Assisi, 142
Frankfurt, Synod of (794), 90–91
Frankish, 57, 61–3, 74, 90, 101, 124
Franks, 15, 53, 54, 56–7, 58, 61, 74, 89
Frederick I Barbarossa (of Hohenstaufen), 107, 125
Frederick II of Hohenstaufen), 107, 115, 128, 129, 141, 142
French
    in period of formation, 61–2
    first written text, 92
    crystallisation, 104, 108–15
    influence on English, 123–4
    later developments, 152–3, 154, 158–60, 167, 168, 169, 170, 171
    pronouns in, 183–4
    other references, 8, 9, 10, 11, 13, 22, 34, 44, 45, 61, 63, 94, 121, 122, 128, 130, 141, 150, 162, 176, 180
    see also langue d'oc/Occitan; langue d'oïl
Froissart, 159

Gaelic, 22
Gallic, 22, 31, 33, 34
Gamillscheg, 33, 57, 61
gender, 9–10
Gerbert, 103
German
    in period of formation, 72–4, 75–7

glossaries, 94–5
    early literature, 79, 95–8
    use of name for, 101
    crystallisation, 124–9
    later developments, 152, 164–6, 168–9
    other references, 9, 11, 12, 13, 16, 39, 40, 42, 102, 116, 130, 182, 186
Germanic, 16, 22, 36–41, 42, 48, 53, 74, 79, 123, 124, 180
Germanic languages, 9, 11, 20, 35–41, 42, 72–7, 79, 80, 89, 91, 99, 151, 180, 181
Gerson, 153
Gervase of Tilbury, 123
Giraldus de Barri (Giraldus Cambrensis), 151
Glaber, Raoul, 140
Glosas Emilianenses, 132
glossaries, 93–5
Gothic, 36, 37–8, 40, 76
Goths, 52
grammar, 10–12, 13–14, 16–17, 174, 177–8
Greek, 8–9, 14, 17, 21, 22, 30–31, 47–8, 76, 88, 151, 177, 182
Gregory the Great, Pope, 68, 97
Gregory of Tours, 31, 43, 68–70, 103, 185–6
Gröber, 32
Guernes of Pont-Ste-Maxence, 113
Guillaume, Gustave, 182, 187
Guinicelli, 142
Guittone d'Arezzo, 142, 143
Gutenberg, 172

Hadewijck, Sister, 130
Hadrian II, Pope, 92–3
Hagendahl, M., 66

Harff, Arnold von, 175
Hebrew, 86, 87–8, 150, 177
Heliand, The, 91, 95
Hellenic, 21
Henry I, King of England, 122
Henry II, King of England, 121
Heredia, Juan Fernandez de, 160
Hermann I, landgrave of Thuringia, 128
High German, 40, 72–4, 127, 128, 130, 165
Hilaire de Poitiers, 87–8
Hildebrandslied, 95–6
Hippolytus of Rome, 86
History of Richard I, 122–3
Hittite, 21
Hohenstaufen dynasty, 107, 125
Homilies d'Organya, 134
Horace, 27
Humboldt, A. von, 34

Iberian, 34
Iberian languages, 45–6, 63–5, 131–9, 150, 160–62 *see also* names of languages
Indo-Aryan, 21
Indo-European, 11, 14, 17–18, 21, 36, 39, 41, 79
inflexion, 11–12, 12–13, 22–4, 28, 116, 127, 169, 185–6
Isidore of Seville, St, 85–6, 87, 88–9, 95, 97
Italian
  in period of formation, 58–60
  crystallisation, 139–46
  later developments, 152, 153, 155, 156, 162–4, 167, 169, 170, 171, 177
  other references, 16, 22, 45, 94, 99, 108, 150

Italic, 21, 22, 79

Jacopone da Todi, 142
Jaime I the Conqueror, 134–5
jarchas, 131
Jardinet d'Orats, 161
Jensen, Nicolas, 172
Jerome, St, 31, 50, 85, 86, 88
Jeux Floraux, 159
John VIII, Pope, 93
John of Brabant, Duke, 128, 130
John of Salisbury, 147
Justinian, 53
Jutes, 53, 74

Kaiserchronik, 125

Lancia, Sir Andrea, 152
Landino, 154
langue d'oc/Occitan, 32, 45, 94, 99, 108–12, 114, 115, 134, 141, 144, 150, 153, 159, 160, 176
langue d'oïl, 32, 99, 108, 109, 112–13, 113–14, 115, 141, 152, 159, 173
Langton, Stephen, 122–3
Latin
  and remote origins of language, 21–2, 22–35, 41
  and period of language formation, 42, 43, 44, 46, 47–51, 54–6, 57–8, 65–72, 75–6, 77, 78
  and meditations of Church Fathers, 88, 89
  and further developments up to early eleventh century, 89–90, 91–2, 93, 94, 96, 97, 99, 100, 102, 104
  and period of language crystal-lization, 105, 106, 108, 109, 115, 121, 122, 123, 125, 129,

131, 132, 133, 135, 137, 138, 139

and later developments, 152–6, 168, 173, 174, 175, 177, 179

other references, 1, 3, 10, 11, 13, 16, 17, 39, 45, 80, 84, 117–18, 149, 150, 151, 180, 184, 185, 186

Layamon, 121, 122

Lettish, 22

lexicology, 8–10, 13, 15–16

Leys d'Amors, 159

linguistic community, 15, 18

Lithuanian, 22

Liudprand of Cremona, 103

Llibre des Feyts de rei En Jacme, 135

Llull, Ramon, 135, 175

Lombards, 53, 54, 58, 59–60

Lot, F., 1

Loth, J., 33

Louis the Fat, 107

Louis the Germanic, 92

Louis the Pious, 91, 96

Low German, 40, 73, 127, 130, 165, 166

Ludwigslied, 96

Lupus of Ferrières, 103

Luther, Martin, 165–6

Maerlant, Jacob van, 130

Map, Walter, 123

Marco Polo, 115

Maurer, 40

Mechtild von Magdeburg, 128

Medici, Piero de', 156

Meier, 33

Meister Eckhart, 128, 153

Menéndez Pidal, R., 32, 33, 35, 133, 135, 137

Methodius, St, 92

Michaelsson, K., 63

Middle English, 104, 122, 124

Middle Dutch, 130

Middle German, 13, 73, 126–7, 130, 165

Millstatt Psalter, 126

Minnesingers, 128

Mohrman, 100

Moignet, Gerald, 183

Moner, Pedro, 161

Montreuil, Jean de, 155

Moors, 53, 54, 131, 176

Moral of Job, 97

Mozarabic, 131, 132

Mozarabs, 55, 64, 99

Muller, H.F., 49

muwassahas, 131

Nebrija, Antonio de, 156, 178–9

Neckam, Alexander, 183

Neumarkt, Johann von, 164

Nibelungen, 126

Nicaea, Council of (352), 47

Niccoli, 155

Nithard, 92

Normans, 93, 98, 106, 120–21, 122

Notker of St-Gall, 96–7, 98, 101, 124

Occitan *see langue d'oc*/Occitan

Old English, 40, 55, 74, 93, 98–9, 102, 104, 115–18, 119, 120, 124

Orderic Vital, 122

Oresme, Nicole, 153

Originum sive etymologiarum libri xx, 85–6

Orthographia gallica, 176

Oscan, 21, 22, 31, 33

Ostrogoths, 52, 53, 58–9, 61

Otfrid of Wissembourg, 95

Otto of Freising, 125
Otto I, duke of Saxony, 96
Otto II, 96
Otto III, 96
Owl and the Nightingale, The, 121

Petit Thalamus, Le, 160
Petrarch, 31, 115, 154, 162, 163, 164
Petri, 57
Philippe Auguste, King of France, 107
Phonetics, 5–8, 12–13, 38–9
Pidal, R.M. *see* Menéndez Pidal, R.
Plautus, 26–7
'Poem of Almeria', 134
'Poems of Clermont', 99
Polo, Marco, 115
Pompeii, 25–6, 29, 31
Portuguese, 22, 33, 45, 46, 48, 63, 132, 133, 134, 138, 160
printing, 171–4
Priscian, 102, 146, 178
Proceedings of Monte Cassino, 140
proto-Germanic, 36–40
Prussian, 22
Pulci, 171

Rathier of Liège, 103
Razos de trobar, 176
Regole della lingua fiorentina, 178
Reichenau Glossary, 93–4
Repgow, Eike von, 128
Rhaeto-Romanic, 22
Robert of Gloucester, 157
Rohlfs, G., 34–5
Roman de Renart, 184
Romance languages
  remote origins, 22, 27, 29, 32, 35, 36, 41

period of formation, 42, 43, 45, 46, 56–7, 65–72
other references, 9–10, 17, 20, 89, 91, 99, 151, 180, 181, 182
see also names of languages
Romanian, 22, 45, 55, 114
Ronjat, 108
Rule of St Benedict, 95, 97
runes, 37

Sachsenspiegel, 128
Salutati, Coluccio, 154, 155
Samson, Abbot of St Edmunds, 122
Sannazaro, Iacopo, 163–4
Saussure, F. de, 4, 5, 13–14, 186
Saxon, 55, 57, 91, 96, 124, 128, 130
Saxons, 53, 54, 55, 57, 74
Scandinavia, 38, 40, 115, 119–20
Schöffer, Peter, 172
Schwarz, 40
'second mutation', 39, 72–4
sermo humilis, 49–50
sermo rusticus, 27
sermo urbanus, 27
Sicilian School (of poetry), 142
Sidonius Apollinaris, 43
Simon de Montfort, 122
Slavonic, 16, 22, 80, 92–3
Slavs, 54, 92–3, 165
Smaragdos, 92
Sordello of Mantua, 115, 141
Spanish, 16, 22, 45, 48, 64–5, 94, 108, 135, 167, 169, 170, 171 *see also* Castilian; Catalan
Spenser, 156
Statutes of Bologna (1246), 140
Straka, G., 46
Strasbourg Oaths, 44–5, 63, 92, 99, 112, 140, 183

substratum, 15
Suevians, 52, 63
superstratum, 15, 58
syntax, 10–12, 24, 28, 39–40, 124,
    169–70

Tacitus, 33
Tassilo, duke of Bavaria, 101
Templar's Rule, 112
Terence, 97
Tertullian, 49
Teseida, The, 153
Tiraboschi, Stefano, 163
Tours, Council of (813), 72, 91,
    101
Trimberg, Hugo von, 129
troubadours, 109–10, 110–11,
    141

Ulfilas, 36
Umbrian, 21, 22, 33

Valla, Lorenzo, 154
Vandals, 52, 53, 63
Veldeke, Heynrijck van, 130
Vielliard, 70
Vienna, Council of (1311), 175

Villers-Cotterets, Decree of (1539),
    160
Viñoles, Narciso, 161
Vippone di Borgogna, 139–40
Virgil, 97
Visconti, Filippe Maria, 152
Visigoths, 15, 52, 53, 61, 63, 85
Vogelweide, Walter von der, 125,
    128
Volume of Vocabularies, 176

Wartburg, W. von, 1, 32, 33–4, 35,
    57, 91, 113
Welsh, 22
Widukind, 96
William I, the Conqueror, King of
    England, 2, 106, 121
William, Duke of Aquitaine, 109
William of Longchamp, 122
William Rufus, 121
Wissembourg Catechism, 126
Wolfram von Eschenbach, 115
Wulfstan, 99
Wycliffe, John, 153

Ximenes de Rada, Archbishop of
    Toledo, 151